Praise for *Cathol.*

"All those involved in Catholic media—not just professionals but any Catholic with a social media account—should be wary of a growing culture of contempt. Jesus teaches us to speak the truth in love, but some of our discourse has become toxic and obscene. In this helpful book, veteran Catholic journalist John Allen shines a light on this harrowing problem and offers a way out. Read this book and learn how to contribute to a culture of compassion."

—**Bishop Robert Reed**, Auxiliary Bishop of the Archdiocese of Boston, President of CatholicTV, Chairman of USCCB Committee on Communications

"When John Allen has something to say, we would all do well to listen. When John Allen has something to say about and to Catholic media, we would be fools not to pay attention. *Catholics and Contempt* is no mere condemnation meant to go viral, a punching down on fake news made by fake people. It offers an invitation, and a challenge, for Catholic media to be better, to strive to create good things, and to recognize the responsibility of sharing the truth of current moments and of the faith. This book is a gift, precisely because it reflects the very best of its author: it is challenging, measured, and sharp. I encourage you to pick it up, learn from it, and apply its lessons."

—**Katie Prejean McGrady**, author and host of *The Katie McGrady Show* on The Catholic Channel on SiriusXM

"John Allen offers a fascinating and insightful read that clarifies the confusion around some of the most explosive stories to have hit Catholic news. He presents a comprehensive lay of the land in Catholic media, provides a compelling perspective into the motives that drive and shape narratives, and calls for a cultural shift from contempt to honesty and respect. It is a timely read as we look for pathways forward that lead to a more healthy and unified Church."

—**Heather Khym**, cohost of the *Abiding Together* podcast

CATHOLICS
& Contempt

How Catholic Media
Fuel Today's Fights,
and What to Do About It

John L. Allen Jr.

WORD on FIRE.
— INSTITUTE —

Published by the Word on Fire Institute,
an imprint of
Word on Fire, Elk Grove Village, IL 60007
© 2023 by John L. Allen Jr.
Printed in the United States of America
All rights reserved

Cover design and interior art direction by Rozann Lee;
typesetting by Marlene Burrell

Scripture excerpts are from the New Revised Standard
Version Bible: Catholic Edition (copyright © 1989, 1993),
used by permission of the National Council of the Churches
of Christ in the United States of America.
All rights reserved worldwide.

First printing, June 2023

ISBN: 978-1-68578-995-4

Library of Congress Control Number: 2022943338

Contents

Introduction

When I'm on the lecture circuit, I like to tell a joke that draws on my upbringing in rural western Kansas (i.e., farm country). To be honest, that part of the world isn't exactly a mecca for the tourism industry. The only time of year we tend to get many out-of-towners is in the fall, because that's pheasant hunting season and some guys like to roll out to the country for a weekend of hoisting shotguns and trying to bag some birds. (For those unschooled in such matters, a pheasant is a large, long-tailed game bird, somewhat like a turkey, and they're common on the high plains.) Generally these hunts involve vast amounts of beer, so often the hunters are a far greater threat to one another than to the pheasant population, but that doesn't stop them from coming.

The joke is set on one such hunting weekend, and it involves a lawyer who's trawling the fields of western Kansas in search of prey.

After a long and frustrating day, the lawyer finally flushes a few pheasants out of the wheat stalks. He takes aim and fires, and he sees one of the birds fall from the sky. He sets off to pick it up, but just as he reaches the spot where the bird has fallen, he comes across a sign that's clearly labeled "Private Property, Keep Out." Since the bird is just a few feet away, however, he decides there's no harm in ignoring the sign and starts to climb the fence. As he does so, the farmer who owns the land rolls up in his tractor.

"Hey buddy, what do you think you're doing?" the farmer shouts.

"That's my bird," the lawyer says, pointing to the fallen pheasant, "and I'm going to pick it up."

"Look, that bird fell on my property, so it belongs to me," the farmer says.

The lawyer loses his patience, beginning to shout threats of lawsuits and crippling legal bills. The farmer smiles and then says, "Well, that may be how you do things where you come from, but around here we settle things with something called the three-kick rule."

Puzzled, the lawyer asks, "What's that?"

"I kick you three times, then you kick me three times, and we keep going . . . Eventually, whoever gives up loses," the farmer says.

The lawyer thinks about it, then decides he's younger and bigger than the farmer and could probably outlast him, so he agrees. The farmer hops off the tractor, the lawyer drops his shotgun and backpack, and they line up eye-to-eye.

"Are you ready?" the farmer asks.

"Go for it," the lawyer says.

Wearing a set of heavy, mud-clod work boots, the farmer gives the lawyer one hard kick in the shin, eliciting piercing screams. He delivers another strong shot into the stomach, causing the lawyer to retch, and a third kick directly into the lawyer's backside, producing howls of pain that could be heard all the way to the Nebraska border. Finally, the lawyer is able to draw himself to his feet and dust himself off. Putting a look of grim determination on his face, he stares the farmer in the eye and says, "Alright, you old coot, now it's my turn."

Smiling, the farmer replies: "No, that's alright, I give up . . . You can have the bird!"

The joke works because we admire the farmer's cunning, and, let's face it, sometimes a swift kick in the backside is precisely what certain personality types need. Yet in reality, of course, such a rule wouldn't really settle anything, because the lawyer would feel cheated and humiliated and likely seek his revenge in other ways, escalating a small dispute over a single game bird into a much larger conflict.

If we look around the media landscape today, it seems we have created a virtual culture dominated by the three-kick rule. In social media, on cable talk shows, in newspaper editorials, and on internet blogs, it seems what drives traffic and lights up the scoreboard isn't a patient search for understanding, but rather cheap shots at people perceived to be political, ideological, and cultural enemies. Pundits and posters have turned into the farmer in that joke, ostensibly concerned with protecting our metaphorical birds but readily willing to sacrifice them in exchange for the chance to inflict damage on people they don't like.

THE RISE OF "CHEAP SPEECH"

Back in 1995, at the dawn of the internet age, political scientist Eugene Volokh of UCLA coined the term "cheap speech" to refer to a new era in which the costs of delivering and consuming information would plummet, creating endless new supplies. Volokh saw "cheap speech" as a positive development, in the same sense that someone might predict that technological shifts would generate "cheap energy" or "cheap food"—that is, that the cost of a good thing will go down dramatically, meaning more people will be able to get it, and many people will be able to afford more of it. Over time, however, as another political scientist, Richard Hasen, has observed, information has become "cheap" in another sense too, meaning "tawdry," "unreliable," "without real value." It's as if, all of a sudden, food costs less, but there are no barriers to putting unsafe products on the market, so we all get sick—or energy costs less but is terribly dangerous, so our appliances blow up.

The reality behind "cheap speech" is that it's opened the door to a tidal wave of hate speech masquerading as reporting and disinformation disguised under a veneer of legitimacy. Although it's cheaper and easier to access information today, one could argue that consumers have never been as poorly informed, divided, and misled as in the early part of the twenty-first century. For one thing, any CFO for a news organization will tell you that reporting is expensive, while opinion is cheap. If you want to document how a particular branch of the government (or, for that matter, of the Catholic Church) is using its money, for instance, you need a financial reporter with the capacity to spend time poring over publicly available financial disclosure forms and seeking leaks of bank records and wire transfers, probably buoyed at some point by the expertise of a forensic accountant. All in, you're looking at spending thousands, if not tens of thousands, on a single story. On the other hand, if you simply want a clickbait piece of opinion saying, "Governor So-and-So is a crook," you can get that for free without breaking a sweat. In an era in which traditional news organizations had the market for information cornered, they could afford to invest resources in stories that wouldn't be immediately usable and profitable; in an era of cheap speech, the incentives for that kind of in-depth reporting just aren't there.

Political scientists such as Hasen will tell you that cheap speech has other corrosive effects, including eroding what's known as the "loser's consent" essential to a democracy, in which people whose side loses an election accept the result as legitimate. As we'll see later, that consent is not only under pressure in the US with the "stop the steal" rhetoric of the Trump crowd; well before that, it took a hit in the Catholic Church with dark whispers of Pope Francis being elected irregularly and

Benedict XVI still being the canonically valid Supreme Pontiff. In addition, cheap speech also diminishes accountability, because when people are trained to see all speech as political, it becomes more difficult to expose real corruption and hold public officials accountable. It also undermines "voter competence," meaning the capacity of an ordinary person to make a rational political choice. That's tough, naturally, when his or her head is swimming with disinformation and demonization.

Perhaps most toxic is the way in which cheap speech has fueled the culture of contempt. In past eras, someone with an obvious axe to grind would have struggled to find the means to broadcast those resentments on a mass scale. It could be done, of course, but it required a certain level of determination and resourcefulness that many people either didn't possess or would choose not to invest in. Today, anger, snark, and derision can be broadcast in real time on a global scale at zero cost. Amid a welter of confusing and contradictory information streams, those outlets and individuals that provide the most provocative content, and the content most likely to confirm user prejudices, tend to be the ones who break through the noise and succeed. Cheap information, in other words, has made all of us cheaper.

THE "CULTURE OF CONTEMPT"

This lust to wound perceived opponents is part of what's often described as a "culture of contempt." The origins of the phrase are a bit difficult to piece together, but it appears its first use in English dates to early efforts at Jewish-Christian dialogue in the immediate wake of the Second World War. Jules Isaac, a French Jewish historian who later played a key role in the document *Nostra Aetate* of the Second Vatican Council (1962–1965) on relations with Jews, referred to a "teaching of contempt" for Judaism in Christianity that, in turn, forged a "culture of contempt" within Christian-dominated Europe. Isaac suggested, and many Christian scholars agreed, this culture helped lay the foundations for the Holocaust.

The first usage of the phrase "culture of contempt" in a more explicitly political context seems to date to Thatcher-era England, where it was first employed by a pair of well-known Anglican thinkers, theologian David Nicholls and Archbishop John Habgood of York, to refer to what they regarded as the contemptuous fashion in which the Iron Lady treated her perceived political opponents. Meanwhile, Thatcher and her allies accused various forces in British society, including the national broadcaster BBC, of betraying a "culture of contempt" in the way they allegedly belittled anyone who didn't share their broadly progressive agenda.

More recently, Harvard social scientist Arthur Brooks has applied the phrase "culture of contempt" to the contemporary American situation in his 2019 book *Love Your Enemies: How Decent People Can Save America from the Culture of Contempt.* A self-described conservative, Brooks described this culture as "a noxious brew of anger and disgust"—not just for an opponent's ideas but for him or her as a person. He quotes Arthur Schopenhauer to the effect that contempt is "the unsullied conviction of the worthlessness of another."

Wherever the phrase comes from, today's widespread culture of contempt is global but tends to be especially prominent in the United States. A mounting body of research in political science appears to suggest that the nation is more polarized than at any point since the Civil War. One such finding is that in the wake of the 2016 election that brought Donald Trump to the White House, one in six Americans—that's a staggering forty-three million people, which is more than the entire population of Canada—stopped talking to a family member or close friend over political differences. Much of that is due to what eggheads call "motive attribution asymmetry," which means that we think our motives are pure and the other side's are evil. Those same eggheads say that levels of "motive attribution asymmetry" in the United States today are comparable to those between Israelis and Palestinians (i.e., really, really high). I don't quite know how they measure such things scientifically, but my gut tells me they're not far off.

When you think the other side is evil, then the proper reaction won't be just dismissal or disagreement; it will be outright contempt.

This culture of contempt is killing us, and not just in the metaphorical sense that it's made our politics dysfunctional and coarsened our democracy to the point where forging consensus around anything is all but impossible. The American Psychological Association has published research that shows that feelings of contempt stimulate the body's production of two stress hormones, cortisol and adrenaline, and sustained high levels of those substances can lead to high blood pressure, heart disease, type 2 diabetes, osteoporosis, and other chronic diseases. It may not be entirely a coincidence that, at a time when adult obesity is a huge health concern in America, cortisol is also known to stimulate appetite and to signal the body to shift the metabolism to store fat. Both physically and spiritually, in other words, contempt is toxic.

WHERE DOES IT COME FROM?

To some extent, the roots of today's culture of contempt may be technological. Every seismic technological shift has important cultural ramifications, and the rise of the internet and social media platforms is no exception. For one thing, the internet has removed all filters to communication, so that people can now instantly broadcast their thoughts about anything to a global audience, encouraging unreflective hair-trigger reactions. For another, digital media encourage anonymous communication; as the old saying goes, "On the internet, nobody knows you're a dog." Experience shows that people will say terrible things anonymously that they would never dare utter face-to-face, and thus, in a sense, social media is designed to bring out the worst angels of our nature.

Technology drives the culture of contempt in another sense, due to the rise of complex digital algorithms that allow content to be driven to users based on their personal preferences. If someone goes online these days and reads one liberal website, algorithms dictate that more liberal offerings will appear in their search engines, in pop-ups that accompany the user wherever he or she migrates, and so on. Further, these algorithms are designed to drive traffic toward conflict, because online slugfests are perceived to elicit deeper engagement from users and thus to expose them to more digital advertising. One 2014 study found that Facebook promotes what the authors called "emotional contagion" because its algorithms favor content that produces an emotional response in the user, with the aim of keeping them on the platform as long as possible. Social media algorithms also are designed to prioritize content that draws high levels of engagement without any consideration as to whether that content is responsible or even true, which is likely why a 2016 study found that false information spread six times more quickly on Twitter than the truth. A 2017 Japanese study found that people of differing viewpoints only rarely discuss issues that overlap; more commonly, a Trump supporter may be following the latest breakdown in the immigration system, while Trump opponents chew over the latest data on climate change. Social media algorithms, whether we're talking about

Twitter's "who to follow" feature or YouTube's "watch history," tend to drive users deeper into discussions dominated by only one point of view.

An article in the November 2021 issue of the journal *Trends in Cognitive Sciences* put the consensus among researchers this way: "Although social media is unlikely to be the main driver of polarization," they concluded, "we posit that it is often a key facilitator." Confirming the point, a now-famous March 2020 study by the American Economic Association found that subjects who stayed off Facebook for an entire month exhibited "significantly reduced polarization of views on policy issues," even if basic differences rooted in partisan identity didn't disappear. (That's actually good news, by the way. The solution to polarization and tribalism can't be eliminating difference, reducing everything to a mushy lowest common denominator. Instead, it has to lie in the capacity to affirm one's own identity while, at the same time, remaining open and nonjudgmental about others. We'll have more about this later, but a compelling role model in that regard is St. John Paul II, whose Catholic identity was rock-solid but who also demonstrated a remarkable gift for dialogue.)

Another piece of the puzzle is sociological and demographic. In 2004, American journalist Bill Bishop began using the phrase "The Big Sort," which later became the title of his landmark book. Using sociological and demographic data, Bishop demonstrated that America was becoming a nation of gated communities of both the physical and the virtual sort. The dominant trend in American sociology, Bishop suggested, was an accelerating tendency for people to live, work, recreate, and even worship only with people who think like themselves. Ironically, as America becomes more and more diverse overall, our neighborhoods, social circles, markets, and even media platforms are becoming steadily more homogenous, designed to appeal not to a broad cross-section but to a narrowly defined niche.

If there's one consistent finding from decades of sociological research about the effects of this sort of physical and psychological segregation, it's this: homogenous communities radicalize; heterogenous communities moderate. In a homogenous environment in which everyone basically agrees on the core ideas, the social rewards come from stating ever more emphatic and radical versions of those core ideas. In more mixed environments marked by constant tensions over core ideas, the social rewards tend to flow to those with the capacity to forge consensus and to defuse conflict. It's no accident that at the same time Americans have been cocooning themselves ever more deeply into what marketers call their "affinity communities," the country is also reaching new heights of polarization and mistrust.

There's also, inevitably, an economic factor to the rise of the culture of contempt. Almost twenty years ago, the late novelist Michael Crichton, of *Jurassic Park* fame, published a novel called *State of Fear*, the central thesis of which was that the military-industrial complex famously described by President Dwight Eisenhower at the peak of the Cold War has been supplanted as the dominant unseen force in American life by a new "politico-legal-media" complex, which thrives by creating a perpetual state of fear. The novel was deeply controversial, mostly because the example of an artificial fear Crichton chose was global warming, and, of course, there's abundant evidence that concern about a warming earth and its potential consequences isn't actually artificial at all. Yet if you take the word "fear" and swap it out for "rage"—and, of course, the two are related—Crichton's diagnosis seems a prescient way of describing the current situation. In the early twenty-first century, perhaps the greatest boom industry of all is the manufacture and sale of outrage, fueled by a 24/7 cycle of punditry on television and in digital media constantly reminding consumers of why they ought to be angry at someone or something, often by amplifying the voices of politicians and lawyers with a similar vested interest in stirring the pot.

As part of the Big Sort, Americans have come to rely on media outlets selected on the basis of ideological affinity for most of their news, which creates a clear economic incentive for journalists to abandon the traditional values of fairness and objectivity and to instead frame stories in ways their audiences are likely to favor. To put the point more bluntly, making people mad is a good business model. It drives traffic, sells ads, and puts money in the bank. The financial rewards for trying to be a voice of reason and moderation in this environment are far less clear. Media organizations that take a clear party line can rely on a dedicated audience willing to pay for their product, as well as the support of powerful and deep-pocketed foundations and patrons. Platforms that don't have such a partisan affiliation struggle to find similar means of support, since the problem with moderates is that few of them are truly passionate about their moderation.

A century ago, G.K. Chesterton mockingly defined journalism as "largely consisting of saying 'Lord Jones is Dead' to people who never knew that Lord Jones was alive." Today, we might say it's the fine art of saying "Lord Jones is a jerk" to people who already thought so but are thrilled to have it confirmed.

THE CATHOLIC SCENE

That's the broad social landscape, but what about the Catholic component?

In general, the Catholic Church understands itself to be an evangelizer of culture, striving to transform whatever society it's in through the lens of the Gospel. Yet in many ways the Church is also evangelized by culture, often unconsciously absorbing assumptions, priorities, and patterns of behavior from the surrounding cultural milieu. Today's prevailing culture of contempt is a good case in point, because we see it in a distressing range of Catholic media platforms and individual

Catholic commentators too. In some ways, the Church has reproduced these broad social trends within its own fold, and with exacting fidelity.

If that all seems abstract, let me offer a concrete case in point drawn from my personal experience.

First, some background. In 2019, my now ex-wife asked me for a divorce. After discussing the matter, we agreed to file for divorce in the state of Colorado, which is where we lived at the time. Our separation was entirely amicable, and we remain good friends. Subsequent to that decision, I began dating a longtime friend and colleague in Rome who was also a coworker at Crux, and we eventually decided to get married. After obtaining an annulment from my previous marriage, which was not conducted in the Catholic Church (my ex-wife is not Catholic), Elise and I were married on January 25, 2020.

As this situation was unfolding, a well-known Catholic pundit named Michael Voris, who founded the conservative platform Church Militant, published a column in which he suggested I had "dumped" my wife and "shacked up" with another woman, charged that I was "objectively committing adultery," and accused me of "willful sin." Because I was living in blatant contradiction to Church teaching, he wrote, my analysis on issues in Catholicism was not to be trusted.

As the old saying goes, everyone is entitled to his own opinion, but not to his own facts. Voris is obviously entitled to his own point of view about the quality of my analysis, and God knows there are days when even I question my judgment. However, his column contained a couple of key factual errors and several important omissions.

To begin with, I had not "dumped" my wife. Rather, she had initiated our divorce and it was mutually agreed upon at every stage. In addition, Elise and I were not "shacked up" but maintained separate apartments in Rome and never even spent a night together prior to our wedding. Without going into unnecessary detail, I can say with a clear conscience there was no adultery involved.

It's also relevant to add that I pursued and obtained an annulment in keeping with Church teaching, Elise and I underwent marriage preparation under the guidance of an experienced priest, and we were married in the Church in a Mass concelebrated by four priests, including one who is an academic theologian well versed in Catholic doctrine on marriage, and another who is a priest of Opus Dei, a group not exactly known for being casual about the moral demands of the faith. Voris would have known all of that had he done even minimal reporting for his piece, but he never spoke to me, to my ex-wife, or to Elise . . . or, so far as I could tell, to anyone else involved. My impression is that Voris picked up a rumor from someone in Rome and wrote it up without doing any of the fact-checking that, not so long ago, would have been required for such a directly personal attack to be published.

In reality, it seemed clear the aim of the column was not dispassionate reporting, but rather wounding perceived professional and ideological rivals. In all honesty, Elise and I were actually something akin to collateral damage, since the column appeared not long after I was named a Fellow at the Word on Fire Institute created by Bishop Robert Barron. I did a Q&A book with Barron in 2017 titled *To Light a Fire on the Earth*, exploring his approach to drawing people to the faith. Voris is not a Barron fan, repeatedly attacking him for being, in Voris' words, "infected with modernism" and promoting what Voris derides as "Catholicism lite."

His conclusion in the column about my alleged infidelity was telling: "This tidy little arrangement between Allen and Barron calls into serious question Barron's legitimacy."

In other words, this was contempt masquerading as journalism. Elise and I got lucky, in the sense that many of our colleagues in the English-language press know us and therefore knew Voris' account to be factually off-base. As a result, no one else picked up the story, and it just sort of died on the vine. Many others we know haven't been so fortunate. Yet I confess that, even years later, it's slightly hurtful that you can still find Voris' piece online, with no correction suggesting there's a problem with the account.

In a sense, it's easy to write off a platform such as Church Militant for its in-your-face extremism. Yet the reality is that Church Militant is no more than a sort of unintentional reductio ad absurdum of the broader realities of much Catholic media in the early twenty-first century. In less extreme and more sophisticated fashion, virtually all Catholic media outlets today in the English language tend to have a clear party affiliation. Consumers know which are the conservative outlets and which the liberal ones, and they tend to craft their preferences accordingly. Moreover, those outlets today often provide greater latitude for personal attacks than previously would have been considered appropriate either on journalistic or Catholic grounds. In addition, many of these reporters and analysts also have an active social media presence, and in that arena, they often engage in contests to see who can deliver the snarkiest put-downs of perceived opponents in a fashion that no serious journalist would have imagined doing not so long ago.

To be fair, it probably isn't terribly surprising that discussions of Catholicism tend to bring out the negative features of modern communications in a particularly concentrated form, since religion generally stirs the deepest passions of the human heart. Catholicism is actually fortunate that so many people care so deeply about the Church's future, seeking by their own lights to push it to become the best version of itself. Yet Catholicism is also called to purify culture, not to uncritically absorb it, and, let's face it, the media culture of the moment is badly in need of some purification.

In a nutshell, that's what this book is about: how Catholics might be part of the solution to the "culture of contempt" rather than one of its striking examples.

Before moving on, let me address an objection to this critique of the culture of contempt that I hear frequently whenever I discuss it, from smart and well-intentioned Catholics on both the right and the left: "Okay, I get it. We could be nicer. But when facing lies, hypocrisy, heresy, and corruption, isn't contempt actually in order? Shouldn't we be bold in proclaiming the truth of the Gospel? I mean, wasn't St. Catherine of Siena at least a little bit contemptuous when she warned Pope Gregory XI that if he didn't use his authority to defend the truth, God would do it for him through all manner of punishments? I'd rather be accused of contempt than cowardice in the face of evil."

Many years ago, I interviewed someone in a conservative Catholic activist group who had been involved in bringing charges of sexual abuse against Cardinal Joseph Bernardin of Chicago, the bête noire of a certain generation of American Catholic conservatives both for his advocacy of a "seamless garment" approach to Catholic social teaching, which critics saw as tantamount to going soft on abortion, and for his Common Ground initiative, which in the eyes of many conservatives sought to make dissent and error as legitimate as authentic Catholic doctrine. Those charges were later withdrawn when therapists judged the accuser's claim of repressed memories about Bernardin unreliable, but we didn't know that at the time of our interview. Among other things, the activist openly described going through the trash of prelates they suspected of either misconduct or doctrinal error, looking for dirt. When I pressed about whether that was just a little sleazy, the answer was something like, "Sure it is, but in the face of evil, you have to pull out all the stops." (By the way, despite the fact that the accuser recanted, Church Militant still has a page describing Bernardin as a "homosexual predator Satanist," asserting, among other things, that not only was Bernardin's abusive behavior covered up, but it often came in the context of Satanic rituals. That's based on the claims of two accusers, without any clear attempt at independent verification.)

Here's my response: Yes, evil merits contempt, but people don't. People must always be respected for their inherent dignity, however wrongheaded they may be on particular points. Moreover, I've been a professional communicator for the better part of thirty years, and I've rarely seen a situation in which shouting "You're evil!" at someone changes hearts and minds. Indeed, styling opponents as malicious usually has more impact on the persons leveling the accusation than on the accused, turning the former into nasty and embittered people incapable of acknowledging the genuine good that so often coexists with error and sin. St. Thomas Aquinas famously said that every virtue carries a corresponding vice, which is what you get when you push the virtue too far or exalt it above all the others. In that sense, we could say that the culture of contempt is a vicious distortion of boldness in defense of truth, not its logical conclusion, and, like every other vice, it festers if left unaddressed. So, let's address it.

Before proceeding to do just that, I need to put a few disclaimers on the record.

First, I believe in objectivity as a journalistic ideal, though I know it's asymptotic; you can get closer to it, but you never actually reach it because, inevitably, one's experience and outlook and sense of priorities come into play. As Hunter S. Thompson once memorably said, "With the possible exception of things like box scores, race results, and stock market tabulations, there is no such thing as Objective Journalism. The phrase itself is a pompous contradiction in terms."

Anyway, on the subject of the Catholic press, I can claim no objectivity whatsoever, because I'm the dictionary definition of an insider. I published my first article in the *National Catholic Reporter* when I was thirty, and I'm fifty-seven today, so I've been covering the Church for the better part of thirty years. Although I do occasional TV bits for CNN as their Senior Vatican Analyst and had a brief run as an Associate Editor with the *Boston Globe*, the vast majority of my work has been for explicitly Catholic media platforms: first NCR for seventeen years and then, for the last eight years, with my own news organization, Crux. I believe deeply in the mission of the Catholic press, and I have strong views about what's gone wrong and what needs to change. All this is deeply personal, in other words, and while I'll try to be as fair as possible along the way, I can't pretend to be dispassionate.

As a related point, I should also add that I have a clear financial interest in this discussion. My platform, Crux, was founded as an experiment in nonpartisan Catholic journalism, and, obviously, should more people be persuaded of the case for it, more people might read our site and contribute to our fundraising campaigns. To be clear, Crux is hardly the only example of responsible Catholic journalism out there, and we don't always live up to our own aspirations. Were the environment in Catholic media to shift without Crux reaping any direct financial benefit, I'd still be thrilled. Nonetheless, the reporter in me always screams "Follow the money," and I can't deny that a less contemptuous media climate probably would be good for our bottom line.

Second, I just mentioned that I'm pulling up on sixty, and I can't rule out that I'm suffering from the usual malady of people as they age, which is thinking everything was so much better when I was younger and the whole world is going to hell. My disdain for social media, for instance, probably is rooted in age as much as experience; frankly, I probably shouldn't be pontificating on the dynamics of social media at all, since I spend as little time in that world as possible. So, if much of this strikes you as the grumblings of an old fogey, you may not be entirely wrong.

Third, I'm often a perfect example of the "Do as I say, not as I do" rule. Over the years, many people who have read my work or seen me on TV or in person at a speaking gig have observed that I can come off as awfully contemptuous of people I think are promoting contempt. Many years ago, for example, I coined the phrase "Taliban Catholics" in a talk at the University of Dallas to describe what I called "a distorted, angry form of the faith that knows only how to excoriate, condemn, and smash the TV sets of the modern world." I didn't name anyone specifically, but both on the UD campus and in wider Catholic conversation, many people seemed to think I was talking about them—and, in some cases, they were probably right. The phrase produced backlash, hard feelings, and deeper division, which in some circles linger to this day—precisely the opposite, in other words, of the outcome I was allegedly trying to promote. It was a great soundbite, but it stoked the Catholic culture of contempt. I've regretted it ever since, but that's another unfortunate thing about the internet: once something is out there, it stays there forever.

I can be my own worst enemy in another sense too, in that I have a pedantic streak a mile wide, and I have a tendency to think that the mere display of obscure information somehow amounts to wisdom. I can come off as annoyingly professorial, suggesting that anyone who doesn't see things my way is that student in the back of the class who's just a little bit slower than the smart kids. To imply that disagreement is equivalent to stupidity, needless to say, doesn't do a great deal to counteract the culture of contempt either.

All that said, I'm going to forge ahead anyway, because what's at stake is simply too important.

As a Catholic, it's always painful to have to acknowledge that the Church has failed to live up to its mission to be the sacrament of the kingdom of God on earth. We've been forced to that realization by the clerical sexual abuse scandals, for instance, and facing the ugly truths of those scandals remains a work in progress. In a similar fashion, we also must face the hard truth that in the division, tribalism, acrimony, and resentment Catholics often show for one another, especially in the digital realm, we also fail to be that sacrament of the fundamental unity of the human family. We should feel the same sense of urgency about reform in facing the culture of contempt as we do regarding the distorted clericalism, institutional defensiveness, and moral laxity that produced the abuse crisis.

You don't have to be a Catholic believer, however, to regard the Church's internal culture of contempt as worrying. To employ the categories made famous by Harvard political scientist Joseph Nye, the Catholic Church is arguably the world's most important "soft power," leading not by force of arms or economic might, but rather by the power of its ideas and its example. Catholicism is the lone institution nurtured in the West that is today truly global, with two-thirds of its membership of 1.3 billion people now found in the southern hemisphere. Further, the Catholic Church is also the largest nongovernmental provider of charitable and humanitarian assistance in the world. To take just one example, it's estimated that the Church delivers 25 percent of all AIDS treatments worldwide, a share that can rise to 50 percent or more across much of sub-Saharan Africa. Countless such contributions add up to the Catholic Church being an enormous force for good and, given the Church's demographics, one of the few institutions capable of promoting real global solidarity.

The bottom line is that, believer or not, we all have an interest in seeing the Catholic Church reach its full potential. The Church cannot do so, however, as long as a large share of its energy and resources is devoted to tearing other Catholics down.

The media did not create this culture of contempt, and we're not uniquely responsible for sustaining it. No solution will be complete if it focuses exclusively on media platforms, ignoring all the other arenas in which rancor and resentment bubble up these days—above all, of course, the individual human heart. Nonetheless, the media is the focus of this book because it's the world I know best, and it also has an outsized responsibility in shaping Catholic attitudes and public behavior.

Another stipulation: By "media" in this book, I mostly mean news organizations and platforms, not individual users of social media and not producers of other forms of media content. I won't be covering Catholic evangelization outlets, for example, or Catholic entertainment sites, or writers on spirituality, theology, or other specialized Catholic interests, except as they intersect with news coverage. It tends to be matters of news interest that produce the most intensely polarized attitudes and reactions, and it's often discussion of news stories that generate the greatest rancor.

Let me sketch what you'll find in the pages to follow.

We begin with a basic mission statement for the Catholic press, because it's impossible to evaluate how we're doing if we don't know what it is we're trying to accomplish in the first place. To be clear, there is no set of commandments for Catholic media that came down off a mountain carved into stone by the finger of God. Crafting a mission statement is a subjective enterprise, and there's no doubt that if I got ten Catholic journos into a room and gave them my version, they'd wordsmith it to such an extent that it would be almost unrecognizable when it came out on the other end. Nevertheless, it's important for me to lay out my vision of the role the Catholic press can and should play, because that will make the analysis to follow far clearer—and, anyway, the aim of this book isn't to close a conversation; it's to open one.

Next, I offer a broad survey of the landscape in the Catholic press today, looking not just at the United States but the global situation. That bit of global perspective is important, and not just for the empirical reason that the vast majority of movers and shakers in the Catholic Church aren't American and aren't getting their news exclusively, or even primarily, from American outlets. Although it's a fact of life that American Catholics represent only 6 percent of the global Catholic population of 1.3 billion today, you'd never know it from much American discussion, which tends to assume that our experiences, perspectives, and instincts are normative for the entire world. It's par for the course here in Rome, for instance, for me to run into Catholics who read the *National Catholic Reporter* from the US or *La Croix* from France along with *Avvenire* and the other Italian Catholic media; to be honest, I rarely run into American Catholics who are reading *Avvenire* along with whatever American platforms they use. Simply as a matter of understanding the Church, therefore, it's good for Americans to be exposed to what the rest of the Catholic world is reading and watching.

Much of the rest of the book is composed of case studies, meaning specific stories that have arisen over the years, how the Catholic press has handled them, and what sort of reactions those stories have generated based upon the way they were shaped by various reporters and commentators. The aim here is not to single anyone out as uniquely responsible for the culture of contempt. No questionable judgment I'll describe in these case studies is something that, on a bad day, I wouldn't be capable of myself. Things would be much simpler if it were a matter of bad people knowingly pushing us down a path of self-destruction, but the reality is that it's more often people driven by noble motives and trying their best to serve the greater good.

Before moving on, a quick explanation about how these case studies were chosen. We begin with the infamous Boffo case in Italy because it set the paradigm for much that would follow. Then we address the massively distorting narratives about two popes, Benedict XVI and Francis, that have circulated in some quarters, because from a media point of view the pope pretty much is the Catholic Church, at least in terms of much media interest, and so these narratives are unavoidable. Finally, we close with a couple of examples that hit a bit closer to home, in the sense that they're contemporary and North American, and are representative of a growing share of what's out there. Some readers may object that of the five case studies, at least three come from an identifiably "conservative" platform, while only one stems from clearly liberal quarters. Honestly, that was unintentional; they just seemed the best examples I had at hand. It may also reflect the tendency, however, that while individual liberal commentators can be awfully contemptuous of their perceived enemies, the Catholic left generally doesn't launch its own media outlets in quite the same way the right does—or, to put it differently, many on the Catholic right are convinced that the left already controls the establishment media, so they're more inclined to fund feisty alternatives. In any event, I'm not trying to blame the right for our problems so much as to sketch tendencies that apply, sometimes in different ways, to all Catholic media regardless of editorial line.

Finally, we'll close with a few thoughts about how the Catholic press might counteract rather than drive the culture of contempt. I might as well confess in advance that none of what I'll have to say is particularly original, and none of it adds up to a magic bullet that will make all our problems go away. Again, the press didn't create this situation by itself, and it certainly can't solve it alone. At its very best, the press can simply provide some basic elements for positive social change, mostly the information needed to think clearly about what's happening and a common space where that information can be discussed in constructive fashion. What happens after that, as ever, belongs not in the hands of pundits but ordinary people.

I do want to read an important caveat into the record. This book is intended to raise awareness of certain troubling trends in the Catholic media these days that, for the most part, simply reflect trends in the broader media culture. I do not want that to be taken, however, as an indictment of the women and men who work in the Catholic press, or who cover the Catholic Church for other news outlets. We are all, always, children of our times, but for the most part my colleagues on the Catholic beat are among the most talented, dedicated, and productive professionals I've ever known. Whatever flaws exist in the Catholic media today, they're in spite of the human qualities of most Catholic journalists, not because of them.

That said, after more than twenty years of abject failure in trying to change the polarized climate in Catholic discussion myself, I remain anchored in the conviction that an independent and responsible press is a sine qua non for a healthy society of any sort, whether secular or ecclesiastical, and that good journalism can change the world.

Just a few notes of gratitude before we get underway.

First, I want to thank all those colleagues in both the Catholic and secular press who have helped show me the way over the years, especially my former editors at the *National Catholic Reporter*. When I started out at NCR, the internet was still on the horizon and the paper was a weekly, biweekly over the summer, so there was always plenty of time for the managing editor to tear my stories apart and force me to rebuild them better. Pam Schaeffer and Tom Roberts did an exceptional job in that regard, and they'll forever have my gratitude. I also want to thank my Italian colleagues who took me in when I first got to Rome and showed me the ropes, especially the late, great Orazio Petrosillo, in whose shadow I've always felt I stand. I also want to thank my family at Crux, including a couple members who have moved on to greener pastures, for tolerating my vast aspirations coupled with my chronic inability to manage my way out of a paper bag.

I also want to thank the people at the Word on Fire Institute for making me their St. Francis de Sales Fellow of Media and Communications, and for publishing this book. I should emphasize that the views expressed here are exclusively my own, so if I miss the mark, blame me and not them. Bishop Robert Barron, the founder of Word on Fire and probably America's most gifted Catholic communicator, has done more than just about anyone else to name the culture of contempt in the Church and to solicit creative thinking about what to do about it, and I want this book to be one reply to that invitation.

Finally, I want to thank my wife, Elise, for sharing this journey. Why she would choose to align her fortunes with a curmudgeonly, aging scrivener like me, deeply set in his ways and an antisocial only child to the core—who, according to one fairly contemptuous commentator on the internet, also bears a striking physical resemblance to the character Squidward on *SpongeBob SquarePants*—is utterly beyond my comprehension. She's a great asset for Crux, sure, but to me she's my world, and nothing I do, this book very much included, would be possible without her.

Now, as the Italians would say, *buona lettura*—have a good read!

CHAPTER ONE

A Mission Statement for the Catholic Press

Offering a job description for the Catholic press requires at the outset that we take a position on the age-old debate of what, exactly, the "Catholic" in "Catholic press" is supposed to mean.

At one extreme would be those who believe that the Catholic press should be the fifth evangelist rather than the fourth estate, that its primary mission is to serve the Church's mission of bringing souls to the faith overtly and explicitly. From this point of view, the Catholic press should not be telling "bad news" about the Church, in part because there are plenty of secular outfits that will do so. The Catholic press must be distinctly Catholic, meaning that it must embrace the faith and communicate it as robustly as possible. There's no need to reproduce within the Church the same skeptical, often hostile coverage one finds in other arenas; the Church needs media that want it to succeed, not to fail. Anything less than that, according to this point of view, isn't really "Catholic" media at all.

On the other end of the spectrum would be those who insist that there isn't actually such a thing as "Catholic journalism"; there's only journalism as applied to the Catholic Church. From this point of view, when one acts as a journalist covering Catholicism, one's obligations aren't to the Code of Canon Law or to the *Catechism of the Catholic Church*, but rather to the canons of good journalistic tradecraft. The Church is just another beat, analogous to the White House or 10 Downing Street or the New York Stock Exchange, and the same principles that dictate sound practice on those other beats apply to the Church—accuracy, fairness, objectivity, and a good nose for news being chief among them. Perhaps a reporter or analyst may be drawn to this beat because he or she is Catholic, but once you enter the realm of journalism you need to check your religious allegiances at the door. The Church already has plenty of preachers and paid spokespersons, but the journalist plays a different role that follows its own logic.

To put my cards on the table, I'm essentially with camp number two. Over the years, I've made a point of defining myself not as a "Catholic journalist" but as a "journalist who covers the Catholic Church." When I left the *National Catholic Reporter* after almost seventeen years to take a position as an associate editor of the *Boston Globe* in 2014, I was sometimes asked what I needed to change or rethink to make the transition from working for a Catholic outlet to a secular one, and my stock answer was "Nothing." That is to say, whether working for a specialized platform or a broad general-interest outlet, my goal in either case is exactly the same: to get the story right, without fear or favor, and to be as fair as possible in the process. The only difference is the amount of background I can assume my audience brings. For a Catholic outlet, I may not need to slow down and explain what a "catechism" is, for example, but I definitely need to do so when I'm on CNN. (Frankly, the better strategy in that situation is usually to avoid words such as "catechism" altogether, but sometimes you just can't help it.)

However, my allegiance to the "no such thing" camp when it comes to Catholic journalism comes with two caveats.

I am a practicing Catholic, and, as such, I know that my obligations to the faith run deeper than any professional code of conduct. If there were a real and unavoidable conflict between being a good Catholic and a good journalist, I would be morally obligated to side with Catholicism. However, a quarter-century of experience tells me that's just not the case. Catholic morality calls a person to honesty, fairness, courage, and fidelity, all qualities central to good journalistic practice as to virtually any other endeavor one can imagine. Indeed, I'd go so far as to suggest that the Catholic tradition ought to be a great corrective to many of the ills that plague the journalism business today. In a media culture of snark, for instance, where character assassination is the order of the day, the great medieval theologian St. Thomas Aquinas reminds us of the dangers of what he called *iniuria verborum*, or "verbal injury," considering it at least as grave a sin as physical assault and battery: "If, by his words, the speaker intends to dishonor another person . . . this is no less a mortal sin than theft or robbery, since a person does not love his honor any less than his possessions." Consciousness of the dangers of malicious speech has been strong in Catholic history for centuries. Consider a medieval collection of canon law, for example, that says that if someone has composed material, either verbally or in writing, that assaults someone's good name but can't substantiate the allegations, the violator should be whipped. (I'm sure we can think of one or two media personalities these days who could do with a good thrashing once in a while. That may be one way to fight the culture of contempt, but winning hearts and minds is certainly preferable.)

In other words, while Catholicism doesn't dictate my journalistic practice, it's perfectly compatible with it and, at key moments, actually augments and even corrects that practice.

The second caveat is that while journalism isn't in itself a religious exercise, good journalism is neverthe-less an enormous service to the Church. The obvious contemporary example is the clerical sexual abuse crisis, where it wasn't careful introspection or internal reform that drove the scandal into public view and compelled

Church officialdom to respond. It was aggressive, independent journalism, performing the traditional watchdog function of the press by holding authority accountable. That reporting began with my former employer, the *National Catholic Reporter*, as far back as 1985, and it burst onto the national stage with the coverage of another former employer, the *Boston Globe*, in the early 2000s. This reporting wasn't unflawed, but on the whole, it generated a national and international focus on clerical abuse that has triggered arguably one of the great reforms of the priesthood in Catholic history. That's what Pope Francis had in mind when he said to journalists in November 2021, "[I] thank you for what you tell us about what is wrong in the Church, for helping us not to sweep it under the carpet, and for the voice you have given to the abuse victims."

Good journalism also serves the Church's evangelizing mission, meaning drawing people to God through the practice of the Catholic faith, albeit in an indirect fashion. Those involved in missionary efforts, especially in the developed West, often report that a chronic stumbling block among many people—especially the so-called "nones," meaning people of no religious affiliation, who tend to skew disproportionately young—is that they've been exposed to a series of prejudices and caricatures of the Catholic Church. These are some of the most popular:

- The Church, and the Vatican in particular, are rich and all about money.
- Religious faith generally is irrational, and the Catholic Church is hostile to science.
- The Catholic Church, through its teachings on the nature of marriage, is anti-gay and hostile to the LGBTQ community.
- The Church, principally through its teachings on admission to the priesthood, is also anti-woman.
- The Church, and the Vatican in particular, are interested primarily in power.

It's not the mandate of journalism to debunk these myths; we're reporters, not apologists, and anyway, there are plenty of folks who make doing so their mission. Yet good reporting is, in a sense, prolegomena to evangelization, because reporting is about presenting the facts of a situation—and, in the case of the Catholic Church, the facts are almost inevitably better than the myths many people believe.

For example, it's often stunning to people to realize how little money, comparatively speaking, the Vatican actually has compared to other major global institutions. Its annual operating budget is around $400 million, roughly one-quarter the size of the annual budget of $1.5 billion at the University of Notre Dame in South Bend, Indiana. (As I sometimes jokingly say, Notre Dame could afford to run the Vatican three times over every year and still have money left over for new football uniforms.) In terms of the Vatican's total assets, it's roughly in the $10 billion to $15 billion range. That's not pocket change, of course, but compared to Microsoft's total assets of $300 billion, or AT&T's $550 billion—or, in the nonprofit sector, Harvard University's endowment of $75 billion—the Vatican comes off as a small fry. The reality is that most Vatican personnel live in modest circumstances on salaries that are terribly low compared to what comparable levels of education and experience could command in other walks of life. These are facts, not myths or subjective impressions, and when good journalism includes them as part of the context when reporting stories on Vatican finances, for instance, they help clear away some of the cultural junk that often gets in the way of taking an honest look at the Church. That's not evangelization, but it's an indispensable preliminary to evangelization.

With all that in mind, the aim for this chapter is to offer a mission statement for the Catholic press that treats journalism as its own enterprise, while conscious of the reality that, even standing on its own two legs, good journalism is also consistent with the demands of Catholic morality and a service to the community of faith.

"RELIGIOUS INFORMATION"

The legendary Spanish layman Joaquin Navarro-Valls served as the Vatican spokesman for twenty-two years, from 1984 to 2006, and was arguably over the span the greatest spokesman Catholicism has ever seen. (In one of life's little ironies, my wife and I now live in the same Roman building where Navarro-Valls established his office after his retirement from his Vatican post.) He once made a critical distinction among three primary ways in which the Church communicates with the world. There's preaching, in which agents of the Church directly proclaim the Gospel, both to nonbelievers and to believers seeking to live it more deeply. There's catechism and apologetics, in which agents of the Church, both clerical and lay, try to explain the Catholic faith and to defend it from its critics, who Schleiermacher once called the "cultured despisers" of religion. Last but not least, Navarro-Valls said, is the category of "religious information," meaning the presentation of information about religious organizations that isn't, in principle, theological or catechetical in character but factual and objective. For instance, answering the question "How many Catholics are there in the world?" is not a matter of preaching or catechesis but information. (The correct answer as of this writing was around 1.3 billion, roughly 17 percent of the total global population of 7.8 billion.) Navarro-Valls argued that just as people have a right to hear the Gospel and to expect explanations of Catholic teaching, they also have a right to reliable information about the Church, and it is the role, he said, of people such as himself to provide that information, without the expectation that it's supposed to be preaching in disguise.

That may not sound particularly profound today, but I guarantee that in the Vatican of four decades ago, it was revolutionary, and only someone of Navarro-Valls' unquestioned insider status in the papacy of St. John Paul II could have made it stick. (For now, we'll have to leave aside the debate over how well Navarro-Valls fulfilled his own mandate—that is, how much of the "information" he presented was really spin and hype designed to insulate his boss and the system from criticism—but trust me, the stories are both legion and juicy.)

In a sense, the mission of the Catholic press is an example of that third sort of communication Navarro-Valls identified, in that we are purveyors of religious information. It is not the role of the Catholic press to preach, and it is not the role of the Catholic press to defend the faith when it's under fire. Again, the Church has whole professional classes of people who perform those roles, and many of them do it exceedingly well.

To get concrete, here's how those three levels of communication might respond to news that a priest named X has just been convicted in a secular criminal court of child sexual abuse.

- **Preaching:** "Jesus said, 'If any of you put a stumbling block before one of these little ones who believe in me, it would be better for you if a great millstone were fastened around your neck and you were drowned in the depth of the sea.' X is a sad reminder that sin strikes everywhere, including in the Church."

- **Apologetics:** "While the story of X is tragic, it's important to remember that the vast majority of Catholic priests are innocent, and they're an enormous force for good both for the Church and within their communities."

- **Information:** "X becomes one of just a handful of Catholic priests to face criminal conviction, as data suggests most accusations are never prosecuted. In recent decades the abuse scandals have rocked the Catholic Church in America, which has paid out an estimated $3.2 billion to date to settle abuse claims."

Those are all perfectly valid ways of engaging the news, but they're highly different among themselves, and each has its own integrity because it's responding to a different set of expectations and rules. What's important for Catholics to understand is that each of these modes of communicating is important, and each serves the greater interests of the Church in the long run, however painful it may be to digest in the here-and-now.

CLOSE ENOUGH BUT FAR ENOUGH AWAY

The trick to covering religion as a journalist is to be close enough to the story to get it right, yet far enough away to remain objective. With allowances for countless exceptions, as a rule many media outlets covering the Catholic Church these days tend to err in one direction or the other.

In the celebrated movie *The Shawshank Redemption*, the character Andy Dufresne, played by Tim Robbins, is a banker sentenced to life for a murder he didn't commit. His hobby behind bars—and (spoiler alert) the key to his eventual escape—is geology. Looking back, his friend "Red" Redding, played by Morgan Freeman, at one point says, "Geology is the study of pressure and time. That's all it takes, really . . . pressure and time." Much the same observation could be made of journalism. Mastering a beat, obtaining the knowledge and perspective needed to put breaking news into its proper context, isn't rocket science. All it takes is the pressure of constant, daily attention—what in the old days we would have called "shoe leather"—coupled with the time it takes for that attention to mature into insight.

The problem with much reporting on religion is that as a rule, and allowing for plenty of notable exceptions, many mainstream news outlets simply don't afford reporters either the capacity to apply sufficient pressure to the beat, or the time it takes for that pressure to add up to real knowledge. Outside Italy, where every major news outlet has at least one full-time beat reporter on the Vatican, and many have whole teams coordinating their Vatican coverage, most mainstream news outlets cover the Church and the Vatican only episodically. Many of these reporters do terrific work when they dip into a story, but because they can't maintain that level of attention all the time, their reporting is often shorn of context and perspective, and inevitably, therefore, tends to overhype certain points and ignore others that are actually important.

To take a relatively silly example, consider the "dogs in heaven" fiasco of 2014. On December 11, 2014, the *New York Times*, America's paper of record, published a story with the irresistible headline "Dogs in Heaven? Pope Francis Leaves Pearly Gates Open." The gist was that during a public audience at the Vatican on November 26, Pope Francis encountered a young boy whose dog had just died and consoled him by saying, "Paradise is open to all of God's creatures"—meaning, of course, that one day the boy would see his pet again in the next life. That story caused an avalanche of reaction, including learned essays by theologians unpacking the significance of the pope's declaration. Upon examination, however, it turned out that the story was bogus. Pope Francis never said any such thing, and certainly not on November 26.

How did this happen? Peeling back the onion, it seems that a write-up of the pope's audience that day, in which he talked about the "transformation of all creation" at the end times, in the Italian outlet *Quotidiano Nazionale*, speculated on what Francis might have had in mind. Along the way, the writer quoted Pope St. Paul

VI decades ago as telling a young boy who had lost his dog, "One day we will see our pets in the eternity of Christ." Next, *Corriere della Sera*, which is more or less the *New York Times* of Italy, published a piece by its highly respected Vatican correspondent Gian Guido Vecchi in which he also recalled the story about Paul VI. The clickbait headline of that article was "The pope and pets: Paradise is open to all creatures." While the article made it clear the pope in question was Paul VI, the headline didn't, and so many Italian websites and media outlets immediately began running the story that Francis had flung open the doors of heaven to Fido. From there, it was a short stop to the British press and, finally, into the *New York Times*.

In all fairness, the reporter on the story wasn't the *Times'* Rome correspondent—at the moment, the position was in flux—but Rick Gladstone, who works on the international desk. Gladstone did a great job collecting reactions from groups such as the Humane Society and People for the Ethical Treatment of Animals but apparently didn't stop first to ask whether the reporting he'd seen was accurate. Though I've never spoken to Gladstone about the faux pas, I've been in similar situations myself over the years, and I suspect my answer would have been something along the lines of "Nothing seemed wrong, and I just didn't have the time to press any harder."

A decent Vatican beat reporter almost certainly wouldn't have made that mistake, and not because they're any smarter or more dedicated, but simply by virtue of time. First of all, a beat reporter probably would have been following the audience that morning and would have known for her or himself what the pope said. If not, such a sensational claim about what the pope said would have driven a beat reporter back to the original sources, in this case news reports written in Italian—which a Vatican beat reporter would have been able to handle easily, since basic fluency in Italian is essentially a job requirement. Note that the difference between swallowing this red herring and sniffing it out in advance isn't about talent but time. Most mainstream reporters simply don't have the time to develop any real expertise on the religion beat and hence are constantly at risk of taking head-fakes such as the "dogs in heaven" story.

Part of that picture is the overall reduction in the workforce in mainstream media over the last couple of decades. In 2020, the Pew Forum found that news-room employment in the United States had dropped 26 percent since 2008, for an overall loss of about thirty thousand jobs. Those reporters who remain are inevitably stretched thinner, making it even more difficult to concentrate on any one beat for an extended period. Part of it, too, is that some mainstream news organizations just don't seem to take religion seriously as a specialized beat in its own right. Over the years it's often amazed me that a news outlet would never dream of sending someone to cover the White House who has no background or awareness of politics, and would never dispatch a reporter to cover the local football team who has no appreciation for sports, but seems to have no problem assigning someone to cover a religion story who has no background in religious affairs at all. God knows—and I mean this literally, given the subject matter—you don't have to be a believer to be a terrific religion reporter, in the same sense you don't have to be a fan to cover sports. What you do need is the time to get the story right, however, and many reporters these days just don't have it.

To take the Vatican as a particularly acute example, I've always said to cover the place adequately requires competence in at least three foreign languages.

Italian: Despite the Vatican's pretense of being a global institution, it's one of the most stubbornly monolingual environments on earth. News conferences are in Italian, the daily news bulletin is in Italian, most documents are released only in Italian (at least initially), and when the pope speaks, it's almost always in Italian. Want to call a Vatican office for a piece of information? You'd better speak Italian. Want to interview a Vatican official who's not from an English-speaking country? Almost inevitably, it's going to be in Italian. When I first got to Rome, I assumed the Vatican would be like the UN and learning the language would be a hobby. (My Italian was so bad when I got here that I thought "prego" was a brand of spaghetti sauce.) I soon learned it's actually a sink-or-swim proposition.

Catholic: As Pope Emeritus Benedict XVI has observed, Catholicism is a culture, and like other cultures, it has its own language. To cover this beat, a reporter needs at least a little bit of background in theology, liturgy, canon law, and Church history, just to cover the basics in order to "speak Catholic." To this day, I remember vividly a news conference with then-Cardinal Joseph Ratzinger, the future Benedict XVI, in August 2000, when the controversial document *Dominus Iesus* on the relationship between Christianity and other religions came out from Ratzinger's Congregation for the Doctrine of the Faith. During the news conference, Ratzinger launched into an *obiter dictum* on competing Jesuit and Dominican views of grace during the sixteenth century. As Ratzinger waded steadily deeper into the weeds, I looked over at the reporter sitting next to me who had just arrived in Rome from the States and whose last assignment had been covering city hall. He stared at me with a classic "deer caught in the headlights" expression, because we were speaking a language he just didn't understand.

Vaticanese: The Vatican, too, is its own culture, and here, too, there's a language all its own. To grasp the dynamics of the place, for instance, you have to know the difference between a congregation and a council—in general, the former are more important and powerful than the latter. You have to know the difference between a *motu proprio* and an apostolic exhortation—the former makes law, while the latter makes arguments. You also have to know the difference between the *sostituto* and a *segretario*, between an *adetto prima classe* and one that's *seconda classe*, and a papal trip that's a state visit and one that isn't. You need to know that when a Vatican insider asks you "Di che parrocchia sei?" (What parish are you from?), he's not really inquiring about which parish you attend for Sunday Mass. He means "What circle of influence do you belong to? Who's your sugar daddy?" None of this language acquisition requires any special mental acuity, but it does demand time on task.

News outlets either unable or unwilling to apply the pressure and time needed to get the story right end up being too far away. It's hard to know, however, whether that's better or worse than the other end of the spectrum, which is being too close to remain objective.

By being "too close," I don't necessarily mean being on the institutional payroll, in the way that, say, *Avvenire* is in Italy, or the Katholische Nachrichten-Agentur ("Catholic News Agency") is in Germany. Naturally, being financially dependent on the institution one's trying to cover can be dicey, but the reality is that each of those outlets I just mentioned regularly supplies terrific reporting and analysis on the Church. In general, that's because the bishops' conference in each of those nations has adopted a hands-off policy when it comes to editorial control, rightly judging that the net effect will be to promote quality journalism about the Church that's taken seriously across the media spectrum and in the court of public opinion—even if, on a given day, there's bound to be a bishop or two with his nose out of joint about something they've published.

The real danger of being "too close" cuts across the dividing line between official and independent media. It's instead about feeling too strong a stake in a religious group's internal tensions and debates, and thus allowing the editorial line of the news outlet to creep into the news reporting. As a general truth about journalism, I always get nervous when I sense that a particular reporter has an agenda, because that's usually a surefire prescription for news that's skewed in one way or another. That danger probably is especially acute when it comes to religion, because religion tends to stir the deepest passions and, correspondingly, the most intense animosities.

Surveying the Catholic media landscape these days, most outlets have a fairly clear editorial agenda. In the US, for example, the country's 70 million Catholics wouldn't all agree on very much, but those who pay attention could almost certainly find consensus in saying that the *National Catholic Reporter*, my old home, is clearly on the left wing of most Catholic debates, while the Eternal Word Television Network, the media empire founded by the feisty late Mother Angelica, is on the right. In other countries, the ideological distinctions aren't always quite that sharp, but if you look closely, they're real enough. Of course, not every reporter for these outlets allows those biases to color his or her reporting, and it must be said that both NCR and

EWTN often do remarkably good work. Nevertheless, there often is a "good guys vs. bad guys" tone to much Catholic news that, inevitably, skews impressions of what's really going on. As noted in the introduction, that may be no more than the Catholic press absorbing the broader cultural orientation of the day, which promotes extremism and discourages balance, but that doesn't make it any less the case.

As a footnote, my own media outlet, Crux, is a bit of an outlier with regard to the bigger picture. We began life as a project of the *Boston Globe*, and although I was given complete freedom to cover stories the way I wanted, there's no denying that the overall lineup and editorial direction reflected the basic, and usually unconscious, liberal instincts of a secular newsroom, and that came across in our coverage. (By the way, this is another reason why being "too close" isn't just a matter of who signs your paychecks. Anyone who thinks that covering religion for a secular platform means operating without an agenda is naïve.) Since we went independent in 2016, relying on a mix of advertising, sponsorship, and reader contributions to pay the bills, we've tried to be nonaligned, not taking sides in the Church's liberal vs. conservative fights or anything else. The net result, in my experience, is that many liberals think we're conservative, and many conservatives think we're liberal—which, I suppose, is about what one should expect given how the winds are blowing. However, I'm encouraged by the size of our readership, which is remarkable given the small size of our staff and our limited resources, all of which suggests there is a potential constituency out there that wants something beyond ideological rancor. Perhaps what it needs now is someone smarter than me, or more charismatic, or both—depressingly, that's a fairly easy combination to find—to figure out how to light a fire under that constituency and change the game.

To cite an example of the dangers of being too close to the story, let's consider the infamous case of St. John Paul II's alleged verdict on the 2004 Mel Gibson movie *The Passion of the Christ*, memorably crystallized in the soundbite "It is as it was."

In December 2003, as Gibson's biblical epic was getting set for theatrical release in early 2004, it was being shown to select audiences in Rome in an attempt to create buzz around the movie in Catholic circles, especially more conservative ones. The screenings were arranged by the Legion of Christ, which, at the time, was at the height of its influence, with the revelations of sexual abuse and misconduct against its founder, the late Mexican Fr. Marcial Maciel Degollado, still a couple of years away. Gibson and his team wanted to enroll conservative Catholics in part to counteract mounting criticism of the movie from groups such as the Anti-Defamation League, which charged it with being anti-Semitic; from Catholic insiders who found Gibson's reliance on visions attributed to Blessed Ann Catherine Emmerich dubious as source material; and from

ordinary folks who simply found the whole thing exces-
sively bloody and distasteful. (Several critics described it
as *Lethal Weapon* meets *The Greatest Story Ever Told*.) Of
course, this was just over a year from John Paul's 2005
death from Parkinson's disease, so whatever reaction he
had would have been communicated through an aide,
most likely then-Archbishop Stanisław Dziwisz, who
went on to become the Cardinal of Kraków after John
Paul's death.

On December 17, a story broke that John Paul
essentially had given the movie a thumbs-up. More or
less simultaneously, Peggy Noonan of the *Wall Street
Journal* and myself writing in the *National Catholic
Reporter* carried a story to the effect that John Paul
had seen the movie and offered a favorable reaction,
quoting the pontiff as having said, "It is as it was." The
suggestion was that the movie is a faithful depiction
of the events narrated in the Gospel accounts of Jesus'
suffering and death by crucifixion. Both stories were
based on unnamed "Vatican sources" in a position to
have been privy to the pope's words after the viewing,
which, due to his age and weakened condition, was
staged over two nights, December 5 and 6, 2003.

The news did not sit well in some quarters, especially among Catholic critics of the film, who tended
to be more liberal in their outlook and appalled by
the pontiff's seeming endorsement of Gibson, a traditionalist Catholic supportive of far-right causes. It also
raised some hackles in the Vatican, where the idea of the

pope appearing to endorse a commercial movie didn't sit well. Over the years, the Vatican had fought legal battles around the world to protect the pope's image and likeness from being exploited for marketing purposes, at one stage even contesting the celebrated "pope soap on a rope." The idea of images of the pope on posters promoting anyone's movie, regardless of the content or merits, drove some in the Vatican to distraction.

The next twist in the saga came on December 24, 2003, when Dziwisz gave an interview to the Catholic News Service flatly denying that John Paul had said anything about the Gibson movie: "The Holy Father saw the film privately in his apartment, but gave no declaration to anyone," Dziwisz insisted. Next, an assistant producer on the film, Jan Michelini, whose father Alberto is a well-known Italian journalist and politician (and a member of the Catholic group Opus Dei, widely seen as conservative), released a statement to me that I published in the *National Catholic Reporter* insisting that he had heard Dziwisz tell a small group after the screening that the pope had said, "It is as it was." Shortly afterward, Noonan published a column saying she had seen emails from Joaquin Navarro-Valls, the Spanish layman who served as John Paul's spokesman, advising producers to use the papal soundbite "again and again and again," even though Navarro-Valls denied the legitimacy of those emails.

Eventually, on January 21, Navarro-Valls put out yet another statement, which, as it turns out, was pretty much the Vatican's last word on the matter. Here's what he said: "After having consulted with the personal secretary of the Holy Father, Archbishop Stanisław Dziwisz, I confirm that the Holy Father had the opportunity to see the film *The Passion of Christ*. The film is a cinematographic transposition of the historical event of the Passion of Jesus Christ according to the accounts of the Gospel. It is a common practice of the Holy Father not to express public opinions on artistic works, opinions that are always open to different evaluations of aesthetic character."

I happened to be in the Vatican Press Office chatting with two colleagues, one Italian and the other American, when the statement was released. After we finished reading it, the reactions were priceless. More or less simultaneously, my Italian friend said, "Okay, that's clear," while the American grumbled, "What the hell does this mean?" It was a classic exercise in Vatican indirection, trying to give everybody a little of what they wanted, and in translation into plain English it meant something like "The film depicts what's in the Gospel, which was the essence of the 'It is as it was' soundbite, and while the pope doesn't make public statements on such matters, I do not deny that John Paul may have passed along a private reaction." For what it's worth, the young Michelini echoed that interpretation, saying, "There never was, nor could there ever have been an official communiqué," but insisted that in a "strictly private and informal" setting, "the pope said he appreciated [the movie] because it represents a faithful transcription of the Gospel." Lending credibility to that reading was the fact that behind the scenes, Navarro-Valls was strongly favorable to the movie and, privately, deeply irritated by Dziwisz's interview.

In the end, nobody was really all that happy: the producers of the film felt they'd been lied to by the Vatican, Dziwisz was irritated that Navarro-Valls didn't simply say "Amen" to his declaration, Vatican old-timers felt the whole affair was grubby and badly handled, and journalists trying to cover the story had a strong case of whiplash from trying to follow all the sudden changes of direction from the various parties purporting to speak for the pope.

Throughout the two-month soap opera, news outlets appeared to break into predictable camps. More liberal outlets didn't want the pope to have uttered the "It is as it was" soundbite because they didn't like either Gibson or the movie, and thus played up developments that cast doubt on the line's authenticity. Conservative platforms, meanwhile, invested in trying to support the film as an antidote to Hollywood's usual treatment of religion, emphasized anything that would appear to suggest John Paul really did say it, or at least that he thought it. In the end, anyone trying to figure out what actually happened without any ideological preconceptions would have been left utterly bewildered, unsure whom to believe. Perhaps the only party to benefit was Gibson himself, since *The Passion* garnered $612 million worldwide, becoming the highest-grossing film of 2004 internationally and the highest-earning Christian film of all time.

Who knows if the reporting would have been any better had people come at the story without any bias for or against Gibson or the movie and simply insisted that Vatican officials get their act together and tell us what was really going on. It's hard to imagine, however, that it would have made things worse, since the "It is as it was" episode would rank on many Vatican-watchers' personal "Bottom 10" of most appalling moments on the beat in recent memory.

TELLING THE WHOLE STORY

Perhaps this is no more than a variant of the "close enough to get it right" rule, but it's a constant frustration how often breaking news stories about the Catholic Church are reported without the context needed to understand whatever it is that's happened. As noted above, stories about Vatican finances are often reported without the dollar amounts involved, leaving people with the impression of Enron-scale shenanigans. In reality, Enron had $63.4 billion in assets at the time it was forced to declare bankruptcy in 2001, meaning more than sixty times the Vatican's asset pool. To take another familiar example, whatever a given pope or the Vatican may have to say about the use of condoms to fight HIV-AIDS, it's almost never situated in the context that the Catholic Church is also the world's largest nongovernmental provider of care to AIDS patients, a piece of information that obviously tempers impressions that the Church is somehow insensitive to the suffering caused by the disease. When covering the child sexual abuse scandals, it's also rarely mentioned that the Catholic Church, through its network of charitable organizations, schools, and health care facilities, probably does more for victims of abuse around the world than any other humanitarian or religious organization. That's not to excuse the abuse scandals, of course, but it does seem a legitimate piece of the larger puzzle in terms of framing public impressions of Catholicism.

One important role of the specialized Catholic media, therefore, is to supply the context that's often missing in other reports. Doing so is not about trying to make the Church look better but simply telling the whole story—although it bears repeating that given the negative light in which news about the Church is often cast, generally telling the whole story does tend to put things in a less condemnatory light.

To get concrete, let's take an example: the oft-repeated charge that the Catholic Church has a "woman problem." The argument can go in several different directions, including the claim that Catholic teaching on sexuality restricts a woman's right to choose, or that the veneration of Mary as both mother and virgin sets an impossible standard for women to try to emulate. Here, however, we'll consider the most common bone of contention, which is that Catholicism excludes women from positions of power inside the Church. (One irony here is that recent popes have been great champions of empowering women in other walks of life, sharply condemning the exclusion of women from positions of political, corporate, academic, and social leadership, but that's a conversation for another time.)

The teaching that women cannot be ordained as Catholic priests has been confirmed by all recent popes, including Pope Francis, who has said that St. John Paul II closed the door, and it will not reopen. To date, Francis has not even acted on recommendations from both a study commission he created and from the Synod of Bishops on the Amazon to ordain women as deacons, a step short of priesthood but still part of what the Church considers "holy orders." In the eyes of many feminist critics, the fact that even a progressive reformer such as Francis seems unwilling to take such a relatively modest step confirms how deeply entrenched the misogynism really is in the Catholic Church.

Apologists for the Catholic faith will sometimes argue that the ban on women priests is not a matter of excluding them from authority, since the priesthood is about service rather than power. The plain fact of the matter, however, is that over the centuries the real power in Catholicism has always been held by clergy, and as long as women are ineligible for the clerical state, there are certain kinds of power they'll never be able to wield. Francis has recognized this reality, saying there's a need for a greater presence of women in the arenas in which authority is exercised, and he's taken steps in that direction within the ambit of the Vatican, but there's always a nec plus ultra built into the equation. If a woman can't be a priest, she can't govern a local parish; if she can't be a bishop, she can't preside over a diocese; and, to take the ultimate case, if a woman can't be pope, then she can't head the universal Church.

The exclusion of women from ordained ministry, and thus from formal leadership, is simply a fact of life about the Catholic Church, and that fact alone always will lead some people to conclude that the Church is hostile to women. Reporters and pundits have every right to make that observation and to pursue stories unpacking the debate over women clergy and its consequences. In telling the story, however, there are important bits of context that often get left out of the picture and that should bear upon any objective assessment of the Church's track record on women.

To begin with, it's also a fact about Catholicism that wearing a Roman collar is hardly the only way to exercise leadership and authority. Historically, some of the most powerful figures in the Catholic story have been women who were never ordained to anything. One thinks, for example, of St. Catherine of Siena, a fourteenth-century mystic, activist, and author who was a member of the Dominican order and who exercised enormous influence on the Church of her day, at one point essentially compelling Pope Gregory XI to return to Rome from his exile in the French city of Avignon.

To take a more contemporary example, the late Mother Angelica was arguably the single most powerful figure in the Catholic Church in the United States during the 1980s and 1990s from her perch at EWTN, a media empire that she built from the ground up at a time when the US bishops were pouring millions of dollars down a black hole in their failed effort to build their own national Catholic television platform. At one stage, Mother Angelica even publicly rebuked a cardinal for his teaching on the Eucharist, and, when authorities demanded she back down, she never really did. If you want to argue that these were both nuns and therefore a highly specialized kind of Catholic woman, then consider someone such as Chiara Lubich, the Italian founder of the worldwide Focolare Movement, one of the largest and most influential of the "new movements" in Catholicism. Lubich was a key counselor to St. John Paul II, and even typically imperious Vatican monsignori would get out of the way when Lubich wanted something.

Moreover, in many leadership positions in Catholicism that don't require priestly ordination, women actually are significantly overrepresented. In the United States, for example, roughly 80 percent of the forty thousand or so "lay ecclesial ministers" are women, a new category referring to lay people engaged professionally in parish ministry. These are the liturgical directors, music coordinators, financial administrators, youth ministers, and others who actually make a parish run, and they're likely to be women.

Drawing on U.S. Census Bureau data, lay ecclesial ministry thus takes its place among the following job categories in the United States, which are most likely to be occupied by women:

- Secretaries/Administrative Assistants, 97 percent women
- Registered Nurses, 92 percent
- Elementary School teachers, 91 percent
- Hairdressers, 90 percent
- Travel Agents, 83 percent
- Lay Ecclesial Ministers, 80 percent
- Waiters/Waitresses, 77 percent
- Cashiers, 77 percent

Women are not represented to the same extent in other job categories in the Catholic Church, but their numbers are generally rising. In diocesan-level administration, 48.4 percent of all positions today are held by women. At the most senior levels in dioceses, 26.8 percent of executive positions are held by women. Arguably, however, that figure should be adjusted, since by definition the diocesan "CEO" in the Catholic system (the bishop), as well as the Vicar General of the diocese, are positions restricted to men. For that reason, women probably hold a slightly higher percentage of senior positions that are actually open to them, perhaps as much as 30 percent.

Perceptions of patriarchal bias aside, the Catholic Church actually does better in this regard than many other institutions. A 2005 study of Fortune 500 companies found that women hold only 16.4 percent of corporate officer positions. Women hold only 6.4 percent of the top earner positions. Similarly, a 2007 study by the National Association of Women Lawyers found that just 16 percent of the members of the top law firms' governing committees are women, and only 5 percent of managing partners are female. According to a 2004 report from the Department of Defense, women held just 12.7 percent of positions at the grade of major or above. In light of this comparative data, the truly interesting question may not be why there are so few women in top administrative positions in the Catholic Church but why there are so many.

To round out the picture, if we put the focus not on who's in charge but who's following them, meaning the typical Catholic in the pew, then the real issue isn't so much the exclusion of women, but rather of men. Below the top levels, the sociological pattern in Christianity has long been a predominance of women, both among church workers and churchgoers. Sociologists Rodney Stark and Alan Miller have studied the religious gender gap, concluding that women are more religious than men by virtually every measure in virtually every culture. While the gender gap is smaller in highly traditional societies in which high levels of religious faith and practice are the norm for both sexes, nevertheless, there's still a noticeable tendency for women to be more involved than men. One estimate suggests that at a given Sunday Mass in the Catholic Church around the world, probably 60 to 70 percent of the people who actually show up are women, and the percentage climbs even higher if we consider daily Mass attendance. As a result, much of Catholic life at the retail level is shaped disproportionately by the tastes, instincts, and interests of women.

In most respects, the Vatican itself remains a male-dominated environment, but then history suggests that major transformations in Catholicism often take shape over a long arc of time at the grassroots before the Vatican ever catches up. As the old joke goes, if you hear the end of the world is coming, head for Rome because it will get there last. Even here, however, the times are a-changin'. Pope Francis has appointed several women to positions previously held only by men, including a voting position in the previously all-male Synod of Bishops, the role of prosecutor in the Vatican's judicial system, the job of deputy foreign minister, and a deputy head of the Vatican Press Office. None of these moves in itself is an earthquake, but together they at least add up to a sizeable tremor.

Does any of this information change perceptions of the Catholic Church as hostile to women? As with most things, the answer probably depends on who's considering it. What does seem clear, however, is that the question never even arises for many people, including plenty of fair-minded folks without an axe to grind, because such context is routinely absent in most reporting and commentary about Catholicism. That's a niche the specialized Catholic press can fill, and if we don't, it doesn't seem likely anybody else will.

A CATHOLIC COMMONS

In the introduction, we discussed journalist Bill Bishop's phrase "The Big Sort" to describe the sociological trend for Americans to cluster themselves into communities of the like-minded, both physically in terms of where they work, live, recreate, and worship, and also virtually in what internet denizens call "affinity communities." That tendency is actually toxic for civic life, because exposure only to people who share common values and worldviews tends to radicalize those positions, while exposure to people who think differently tends to promote moderation. The results are clear from the acutely polarized politics of America today, which, to one degree or another, are often reflected in other parts of the world as well.

Not only is the Catholic Church not immune from these broader forces, but in some ways Catholicism in America has become a leading case in point. The normal pillars of Catholic life often no longer naturally bring Catholics of differing perspectives together. Many parishes, for instance, have essentially become gated communities. Walk into any diocese in America and find a Catholic in the know, and he or she can tell you in five minutes where the "Vatican II" parishes are, the neo-con parishes, the traditionalist parishes, and so on. The same point could be made about Catholic colleges and universities, Catholic media, and other institutions, all of which tend to have clear ideological alignments. Once upon a time, these institutions created a Catholic "commons," where believers of different temperaments and outlooks could rub shoulders and form friendships. Today, however, they tend to act as agents of tribalism rather than antidotes to it.

What to do about all this? In this regard, I like to tell a story about my ex-wife, Shannon Levitt, who remains a close friend and valued member of the Crux team. Back in 2004, I was traveling around the world researching a book on Opus Dei, and Shannon made several of those trips with me. The usual pattern was that while I was out researching, she'd do some touristy thing, usually accompanied by a couple of female Opus Dei members who volunteered to show her around. Shannon, you need to understand, is Jewish rather than Catholic, and decidedly liberal in her politics, so the idea of spending a lot of time with people she perceived as conservative and given to bouts of overt Christian piety didn't exactly fill her with glee. Yet the people she met along the way were unfailingly generous, smart, and funny, and she always had a good time with them.

One day I came back to our hotel in Nairobi, Kenya, and found Shannon obviously melancholy and deep in thought. When I asked what was wrong, she said, "It's these Opus Dei people. . . . I know I should hate them, but they're just so damn nice!"

From that point forward, whenever the topic of Opus Dei would come up in mixed company, I usually didn't have to say anything because Shannon would take point, insisting that whatever stereotypes were being voiced didn't correspond to the reality of the people she knew. What had changed wasn't that Shannon was argued into a different way of looking at a group she was ideologically not disposed to appreciate; it was rather the experience of becoming friends, because she'd been exposed to Opus Dei members not as caricatures or debating partners but as real flesh-and-blood people in nonthreatening environments, and friendship was the natural result.

To me, the conclusion to be drawn from this and similar experiences is clear: if we want to swim against today's tide of polarization, acrimony, and tribalism, then we have to carve out spaces where Catholics of differing outlooks and temperaments can meet one another and become friends. It's not about formal dialogue programs, where people come together and debate their differences, which usually deepens the divides rather than ameliorating them. Instead, it's about natural, organic, unforced, and unscripted moments in which people connect on a basic human level rather than as exponents of a particular position. For that to happen, they need places of encounter. The best option is always face-to-face, in person, but where that isn't possible, Catholic media can also play a subsidiary role in carving out such spaces in the virtual sphere. There's an infinite range of ways in which media outlets might draw people out of their usual antagonisms and provide them opportunities to interact in ways prone to foster friendships. I've often thought, for example, of doing a series with prominent Catholics from the various camps to discuss their favorite meals. Over the centuries, food (and drink, of course) has often been the glue that's held Catholicism together; even when bishops couldn't agree over who was the legitimate pope, they were still able to sit down and share a plate of *bucatini all'amatriciana* while they hashed it out. I see no reason why the dinner table can't come to our rescue again today, and that's merely one possibility. The point is that Catholic media outlets must be intentional about seeking them out.

Just in case you're wondering, I don't see this as a departure from my "journalist who happens to be Catholic" mantra. A good metro paper will always care about the city it covers and will try to serve the needs of the community. Local papers run food drives, promote blood donation campaigns, try to hire minorities and women and other historically neglected pockets of the city, and strive in their coverage to reflect the real concerns and needs of the population. In the same way, the Catholic press has an obligation to care about the overall welfare of the Church, including rethinking modes of coverage and speech that may not serve the

Church's best interests, especially when the Church faces a problem the media has helped to create. Being objective doesn't mean being value-free; instead, it means trying not to allow your values to skew the way you report the news.

Based on everything we've covered in this chapter, herewith my version of a mission statement for the Catholic press:

> **Mission Statement:** The role of the Catholic press is to bring the best practices of journalism to bear on covering the Catholic Church. Specifically, the Catholic press should strive to do three things:
>
> - Be close enough to get the story right, but far enough away to remain objective.
> - Tell the whole story, providing information to put breaking news in context.
> - Create a "Catholic Commons" in which friendships can be formed.

That's not the Magna Carta, I suppose, but it'll do.

CHAPTER TWO

Surveying the Landscape

The Second Vatican Council, a summit of nearly 2,500 Catholic bishops from all over the planet that took place in Rome from 1962 to 1965, was the defining moment for the Catholic Church in the second half of the twentieth century, and in many ways debates over the legacy of Vatican II continue to define the fault lines in Catholicism today. While the liberalizing spirit of *aggiornamento*, or "updating," that swirled at the council was felt in virtually every arena of Catholic life, from the role of the laity vis-à-vis the clerical caste to ecumenism and interfaith dialogue, its impact for the ordinary Catholic was felt most keenly in the Mass. Almost overnight, Catholicism went from celebrating its rites in Latin, in keeping with a centuries-old tradition, to drawing on the modern languages used in everyday speech. So great was the upheaval that a small number of Catholics actually went into schism, meaning a formal break with the Church, over their inability (or unwillingness) to adapt to the new order, seeing it as illegitimate and even borderline heretical.

To this day, the liturgy tends to be a battlefield in Catholicism where even minor proposed changes generate outsized reactions because of their presumed symbolic significance: Are we moving closer toward the vision of Vatican II or farther away from it? (As an example, consider the uproar that emerged in 2010 when the US bishops changed a few of the public responses at Mass, such as abandoning "And also with you" when the priest says, "The Lord be with you," in favor of "And with your spirit." That small tweak generated whole books brimming with learned commentary, biting criticism, enthusiastic support, and old-fashioned wonky analysis.)

Exacerbating the intensity of what wags call the "liturgy wars" is that it's one area of Church life about which every Catholic has an opinion. Most Catholics have never studied theology or canon law, but they've been to Mass, and so they feel entitled to speak up. (By the way, this is the same reason many Americans may tune out debates over tax policy or geopolitics—they've never read the tax code, after all, and they've never been to Ukraine or Pakistan or whatever place is hot at the moment. But they all have an opinion about education policy, because they've all been to school.)

Thus, when Pope Benedict XVI decided in 2007 to widen permission for celebration of the old Latin Mass alongside the newer rite in an edict titled *Summorum Pontificum*, you would have thought the Battle of the Bulge had broken out. Benedict said he was acting to promote unity in the Church by satisfying the desires of more conservative and traditional Catholics to have access to the old Mass, but the resulting bare-knuckles brawl in the Catholic press smacked of anything but unity. That fracas, however, turned out to be nothing but a brief shower compared to the thunderstorm that erupted fourteen years later, in July 2021, when Pope Francis abrogated Benedict's ruling altogether, decreeing that in the future Mass generally must be celebrated in the new, post–Vatican II format, apart from a few limited exceptions, and that there's really no room anymore for the older Latin Mass on the Church's playlist. Once again, the pope claimed to be issuing his ruling, which came in a document titled *Traditionis Custodes*, in the interests of unity, and once again, the public reaction in the Church was anything but unified. Not only did this stir old wounds over how the Mass ought to be celebrated, but it was also a case of one pope directly reversing the decision of another, which raised a whole new set of animosities over papal authority and how it ought to be exercised.

If you read the coverage in the Catholic press of *Traditionis Custodes*, you would have concluded it was one of the most important policy decisions of Francis' papacy and easily the story of the year in 2021. It drew sustained, massive levels of Catholic media interest and attention and was framed as the culmination of tensions in Catholicism that reached all the way back to Vatican II. The story seemed to have everything going for it, including starring roles for the favorite heroes of both the Catholic right (Benedict) and the Catholic left (Francis).

What a disappointment, then, for those of us who make our living in the Catholic press to come across the results of a national poll by the Pew Research Center in October 2021, which found that 65 percent of American Catholics, virtually two-thirds of all Catholics in the country, knew nothing—zero, zilch, nada, *un bel niente*—about what Pope Francis had done on the Latin Mass. Asked how much they had heard about Francis' decision to place limits on the Latin Mass, 65 percent replied "nothing at all."

Let's pause for a moment to ponder that result. The Catholic press, left, right, and center, had done everything it could for a good four months by that point to gin up the pope-reverses-pope saga into a compelling Catholic drama, only to learn that two-thirds of the target audience didn't even know it happened. Perhaps not since Kevin Costner's *Waterworld* has a production flopped so badly with respect to the resources poured into it.

Admittedly, the furor over the Latin Mass may have been eclipsed by the fact that shortly before it was issued, Pope Francis was forced to go to Rome's Gemelli Hospital for a previously unannounced colon surgery, which turned out to be more serious and complicated than initially suggested. Francis didn't return to the Vatican until two days before *Traditionis Custodes* was issued, at a time when many global media outlets, especially secular platforms, were still preoccupied by papal health stories. Still, the Pew results suggest a sobering realization for the Catholic press: we did our best to draw eyeballs to a story, and, statistically at least, we failed massively. Put another way, what the findings suggest is that at least two-thirds of the American Catholic population just isn't paying any attention to the Catholic press.

The hard truth that journalists who specialize in Catholic affairs have to face is that we generate an insider product that most Catholics, most of the time, aren't interested in and will never consume. Even the typical Mass-going Catholic, who shows up on Sunday and volunteers around the parish and gives to fundraising campaigns and prays the Rosary at home, has precious little interest in the vicissitudes of debates over papal leadership or the bishops' conference. Frankly, people today live in a politics-saturated world in every other arena of their lives, and those who go to church on Sundays generally don't want to face it there too. In that regard, a story about my late grandfather may be illustrative.

Raymond Leo Frazier, born in Palco in rural western Kansas in 1912, died on October 25, 2004, in Hill City, also in rural western Kansas. In the ninety-two years in between, he rarely ventured out of that comfort zone, occasionally taking vacations to satisfy my grandma and mom but generally not really caring for it. An auto mechanic by trade, he was the closest thing I ever knew to a truly content person—absolutely everything he needed or wanted was right there in little Hill City, as long as his family was around. He was, in a sense, one of those quiet saints often talked about in Catholic spirituality. He was honest, fair, and compassionate in both his business dealings and his personal life, and while he didn't advertise his religion on his sleeve, he was also a sincere Catholic believer. At one point he served as the Grand Knight of the local chapter of the Knights of Columbus at Immaculate Heart of Mary parish in Hill City, a church he actually helped build earlier in life. He never missed Sunday Mass—admittedly, my grandma wouldn't have let him even if he tried, but he was happy to go—and although he was by no means an intellectual, he nevertheless had a thoughtful inner spiritual life. He was right with God, in other words, and right with the people in his life, and it's hard to know how much more you can ask.

What my grandpa wasn't, however, was interested in the details of my job. I vividly remember one day when I was visiting the family after having been in Rome for a couple of years, and I found myself sitting in my grandparents' living room after Sunday lunch. My grandma and mom were in the kitchen cleaning up, while grandpa and I sat in easy chairs watching a football game. We hadn't been in position too long, so grandpa wasn't yet asleep—sooner or later he'd doze off in front of the TV and have to be awakened for supper.

Since he was trying to engage in conversation, I decided to use him as an x-ray of ordinary Catholic opinion. We're talking about the late 1990s, so St. John Paul II was pope, and I simply put it to grandpa, "Hey, what do you think of this pope?"

His semi-snarky response marked one of the few times I actually heard him vocalize irritation with anybody: "What do I think? He's the Goddamn pope, that's what I think!"

What grandpa meant was that he didn't need to know what the pope's vision was, or the logic for his recent trip to X country, or why he appointed Bishop Y to some important Vatican post. He's the head of the Church, the successor of Peter, and Christ's vicar on earth, so what more do you need? For an awfully wide range of Catholics like my grandpa, including some of the most committed, the answer to that rhetorical question is obvious: "Nothing." To try to get my grandpa interested in the Latin Mass debate would be akin to getting an Alaskan Native interested in a beachwear convention (i.e., a waste of time).

WHO'S OUT THERE?

So, who is consuming the Catholic press? Over the years, I've come to understand our audience in terms of concentric circles. This isn't the statistical result of an empirical media use survey, but simply what experience suggests the basic picture to be.

In the innermost circle would be people who are daily consumers of Catholic news, from a variety of different outlets and in a variety of different languages. (We'll come to this later, but the single most important language in the world to possess in terms of following Catholic affairs is Italian. After that come English, Spanish, German, and French, probably in that order.) Who's in this circle? To begin with, other Catholic journalists, who, for obvious reasons, try to consume as much news and analysis about the Church as humanly possible. To the extent I'm representative, my daily reading list (or, the case may be, scanning list) includes *L'Osservatore Romano*, the official Vatican newspaper (the Italian edition, which is more expansive than the editions in other languages); *Avvenire*, the newspaper of the Italian bishops' conference, which does some of the best reporting on the Church anywhere; *Corriere della Sera*, Italy's newspaper of record; *Il Messaggero*, Rome's principal daily; and a sampling of major Catholic platforms in English, such as the *National Catholic Reporter* and the Catholic News Agency.

Beyond journos, the inner circle includes bishops and priests, though by no means all. It's a persistent misconception many people have, for instance, that a bishop has to know the Vatican well. Whenever a Vatican story breaks, it's the natural tendency of local religion reporters to call the bishop for comment, even though the great likelihood is that the bishop doesn't know any more about it than the mayor or the police chief. If you were to take a survey today of the roughly three hundred Catholic bishops in America, including active diocesan bishops, auxiliaries, and those who are retired, I suspect maybe 20 percent would be able to correctly name Cardinal Pietro Parolin as the current Vatican Secretary of State, and fewer would be able to name his three immediate predecessors—Agostino Casaroli, Angelo Sodano, and Tarcisio Bertone—although each was über-powerful in his time. The truth is, the focus of most bishops is local, at most also national, with precious little time left over for the universal. Most bishops will visit Rome only a handful of times in their lives, usually as part of the *ad limina* trip all bishops are required to make every five years while they're in office. They'll never speak Italian, never have friendly dinners with Vatican officials, and never serve on a Vatican dicastery, and they won't feel their lives or ministries are any poorer for it. Frankly, most bishops I've met over the years have enough grief just trying to get through the day running their own diocese, and they don't need the aggravation that comes from being caught up in Vatican politics.

The same point applies even more to priests. Some have studied in Rome, know the players and the game, and pay careful attention to who's up and who's down, but most, frankly, couldn't care less. Their focus is on their parish or whatever else they're involved in, and they will look up to notice something happening in the Vatican only when it may affect their life or work. (I have a priest friend, for example, who's a medical doctor with a special interest in palliative care. He pays close attention whenever the Vatican or some other Church authority says something related to end-of-life issues, but if you were to ask him what the pope is doing about empowering laity, or the role of women, or liturgy, or anything else outside his interests, he'd draw a complete blank.)

If you want to know how most sleeves-rolled-up pastors think about ecclesiastical officialdom, whether it's the Vatican or the bishops' conference or even his own local chancery, it was crystallized for me early in my career by an elderly Italian pastor at the Roman church I attended back then for Sunday Mass. The president of the Italian bishops' conference at the time, the legendary Cardinal Camillo Ruini, had just issued a letter addressed to pastors providing a detailed series of guidelines and regulations regarding pastoral councils and finance councils in Italian parishes, which was controversial because it seemed to critics an effort to limit the autonomy of those bodies and to reassert clerical authority. I asked my veteran pastor friend what he made of it, and he smiled at me and responded: "Sai, con tutti questi documenti che non si finiscono mai, ormai il segretario migliore per un parroco è il cestino," meaning, "You know, with all these never-ending documents, by now the best secretary for a parish priest is the trash can." Needless to say, this pastor wasn't a big consumer of Catholic news either.

Also in the inner circle would be other "professional Catholics," meaning people whose careers are somehow tied up with the Church, such as people who work in diocesan chanceries or at a bishops' conference; academics who follow Church affairs; officials of Catholic movements, organizations, and religious orders (including orders of both men and women); officials at embassies accredited to the Vatican; officials with other Christian churches or religious traditions involved in dialogue with Catholicism; executives with companies that do business with the Vatican; and so on. These are folks who have a vested professional interest in understanding what's happening in the Church, both in the Vatican and at the local level, and who rely on the media to provide information and analysis they won't get in official communiques. Sometimes they can glean helpful information from the mainstream media too, but nine times out of ten, they rely on the Catholic press simply because we're paying attention every day.

Beyond professional Catholics, there are also some folks in that inner circle of Catholic press users simply by choice, because they find it fascinating or because they're passionately attached to some cause within the Church they want to promote. This subgroup is a motley crew; you'll find Latin Mass aficionados cheek-by-jowl with advocates of women's ordination, though they're usually not consuming the same sources of information. The kind of Catholic who watches the far-right Church Militant news show online every night, for instance, is probably not also reading the left-leaning *National Catholic Reporter*—or, if they are, it's only to find the latest outrage to be mad about. Yet the common term is that, unlike the vast majority of Catholic laity and even clergy in the world, most people in this group probably could tick off Casaroli, Sodano, and Bertone along with Parolin without missing a beat.

Note, by the way, that of all the groups I've mentioned in the inner circle of Catholic news consumption—journalists, diplomats, business executives, academics, professional Catholics, and some bishops and clergy—not all of them are populated exclusively by Catholics. In other words, a good chunk of the most devoted users of Catholic media aren't even Catholic. I've got non-Catholic and even atheistic friends at embassies here in Rome, for instance, who could nevertheless recite the latest developments in a Vatican trial with remarkable precision.

Next out is the circle of what I'd call "occasional" consumers of Catholic news, meaning people who dip in and out depending on what else is going on in their lives and their personal interests. I'm talking about the kind of person, for instance, who maybe has a few Catholic sites bookmarked, or who gets alerts from their choice social media platforms about stories of Catholic interest, but who doesn't feel compelled to consume all that stuff every day. When something pops up that catches their attention, and they don't have anything else compelling to do in that moment, they'll check it out. In this circle you can probably find another chunk of virtually all the groups mentioned above, as well as a relatively small sampling of ordinary Catholics who feel some interest in Church affairs but who aren't driven to stay on top of it all the time.

Where you will find a massive presence of those ordinary Catholics is in the next concentric circle, which is the "big story" consumer. These are people who routinely pay little attention to the zigs and zags of Church politics, but who will check in whenever something truly major seems to be happening. The paradigmatic case in point, of course, is the death of a pope and the conclave that follows to choose a successor. At that point, all kinds of people who don't ordinarily follow such things develop a strong interest and consume virtually everything they can get their hands on, both from the mainstream secular press and the specialized Catholic press. While plenty of non-Catholics will be in this group too, it's disproportionately Catholic because those are the people mostly likely to feel a tug to pay attention.

The last circle (of Catholic press use, not Dante's inferno) would be composed of the general public, Catholic and not, meaning folks who pay zero attention to Church news on a regular basis and who only check in when there's some massive story breaking all over the media that's almost unavoidable. St. John Paul II's funeral Mass on April 8, 2005, for example, was carried live by virtually every major broadcast network in the world, and, to this day, is reckoned to be the most-watched single live event in human history. (I was part of CNN's broadcast team that day, sitting alongside Christiane Amanpour, Anderson Cooper, and Bill Hemmer. When a friend of my grandma in Hill City later asked her if she'd watched her grandson, she replied, in vintage fashion, that the only thing she watched on TV was the weather.) Even if you had no prior interest in Catholic news at all, it was basically impossible not to know that John Paul had died and a new pope was about to be elected, and, in a few cases, that may have driven some of those people to check out a few offerings in the Catholic media while the story was hot.

THE "GRAYBY BOOM"

Another thing that probably should be said about the consumption of Catholic media is that regular users tend to skew disproportionately toward the older end of the demographic spectrum. Every Catholic print outlet I've ever been involved with has, at one point or another, gotten into a panic about internal data showing their readers are getting older, and they worry about that not being sustainable in the long run.

While the concern is understandable, it has to be held in the context of at least three other consider-ations. First, readership for most print products, not just the Catholic press, is in decline, in part because of generational shifts toward consuming news in other ways, especially platforms with an engaging mix of print, audio, and video. While traditional jobs in newsrooms across America dropped sharply from 2008 to 2020, a decline of 57 percent, according to a study from the Pew Research Center, jobs in digital media shot up by 144 percent in the same period. Recently, a researcher at the Walter Cronkite School of Journalism in Phoenix published a piece warning of a critical hiring shortage in TV newsrooms, saying there's not enough young talent to meet demand. The reality may be that the press in general, not just the Catholic press, isn't dying so much as mutating.

Second, the dominant demographic trend in America and all across the West today is a rapid aging of the population—what some wags call the "grayby boom" (a play on the term "baby boom"). In the United States, the median age was 30 in 1950, but it will reach 41 by 2050. In Europe it will be 47.1, and in Japan a staggering 52.3. Fully a third of all Japanese will be over 60 within a decade. The Institute for Health and Aging in the United States reports that in 1990, for every person over 85 years of age, there were 21 people between the ages of 50 and 64. In 2030, for every person over 85, there will be only six people between 50 and 64, a massive shift toward an elder-dominated culture. As the President's Council on Bioethics stated in 2005, we are on the brink of becoming a "mass geriatric society." There will be 75.9 million Americans above 65, as opposed to 59.7

million under 14, meaning the elderly will outnumber the youngest in the country by more than 16 million. The population of "old olds," meaning those above 85, will also increase four-fold.

Periodically, Church leaders will rue these realities out loud as an index of societies that are no longer open to new life and raising large families. Pope Francis, for instance, often laments the "demographic winter" in his own backyard in Italy, which has one of the lowest birth rates in the developed world. At the retail level, pastors and ordinary Mass-goers often find themselves depressed by all the gray heads they see in church, worrying about how to appeal to younger generations. The point for the Catholic press is that it isn't just our audience that's getting older; pretty much every subgroup in the culture one could think of is graying too, and rapidly.

By the way, this isn't necessarily bad news for Catholic media. All the available sociological data suggests that across cultures, the elderly are disproportionately more likely than the general population to take religion seriously and to practice their faith, suggesting they're more inclined to be interested in media platforms that cover their church. In America, sociological data shows that the 65+ group is easily the most religious segment of the population, both in terms of attitudes and practice. A recent Pew study concluded that just 27 percent of US adults 18–34 describe themselves as "religious," as opposed to 47 percent of those 65+. (That difference is also a barometer of religious intensity, since more young adults than seniors choose the "somewhat religious" option.) A Baylor University survey found that 18.6 percent of those 18–30 said they have "no religious affiliation," while the number drops to just 5.4 percent among those aged 65 and up. A U.S. News and World Report / PBS Religion and Ethics Newsweekly survey concluded that 60 percent of those 65+ attend religious services at least once a week, compared to just 34 percent of those aged 25–34. Evidence also suggests that someone who is at least marginally open to religion at 35 is likely to be more so at 65. The late novelist and sociologist Fr. Andrew Greeley once found that an uptick in both prayer and attending religious services begins in the early thirties and builds as people age.

Multiple studies also have found that elderly people are far more likely to read news in print and to watch traditional TV news broadcasts than other age cohorts, which means they're the natural audience for what we do. Further, many elderly people possess the resources to financially support media outlets they value. The advertising firm Martino and Binzer, which specializes in "mature marketing," estimates that Americans over 55 possess $1.5 trillion in discretionary spending. Abundant sociological data also indicates that people tend to get more conservative as they age. "We can say, with a great deal of confidence, that people get more conservative when they get older—and a lot more," says Sam Peltzman of the University of Chicago's Booth School of Business. "It's not just a little bit. It's a pretty big change over their lifetime." Among other things, that implies a greater affiliation with, and interest in, traditional institutions such as churches and synagogues.

To put the point in crass commercial terms, the "grayby boom" is actually creating a potential boom market for the Catholic press, if we have the imagination to seize it. (At a very practical level, for instance, both online and traditional print publications might want to think about increasing the font size in articles, which is a classic complaint among many elderly readers.) If someone were to dream up a PR program for people basically uninterested in Church affairs that drew 6.8 million into potentially greater use and giving for Catholic media within a quarter-century, it would be hailed as one of the greatest marketing campaigns of all time. Today, demographics are to some extent doing the job all by themselves.

Third, the good news is that the Catholic Church already has an abundant set of resources directly relevant to the life situations and interests of elderly persons. St. John Paul II published a moving "Letter to the Elderly" in 1999, which was the United Nations' "Year of the Elderly." The pope's own highly visible frailty in his later years stirred Catholic consciousness. The US bishops published their own pastoral document in 1999, "The Blessings of Age," which states: "How the community relates to its older members—recognizing their presence, encouraging their contributions, responding to their needs, and providing appropriate opportunities for spiritual growth—is a sign of the community's spiritual health and maturity." Pope Francis has made outreach to the elderly a leitmotif of his pontificate, frequently encouraging younger Catholics to spend time with elders in order to absorb the wisdom of experience. That's not to suggest, of course, that elderly consumers of media are interested only in stories about old persons, but it is to say that the Catholic press doesn't have to start from scratch in looking for material to inform its basic outlook and to draw upon in coverage plans.

None of this means that Catholic media platforms should give up on drawing younger users, but it does imply that far from clucking sadly when we metaphorically see a lot of gray heads in our traffic data, our hearts ought to gladden.

WHAT'S OUT THERE?

A perennial challenge for anyone just trying to get up to speed on Church affairs is which news outlets they ought to follow. There's a bewildering variety out there, representing a welter of different and often competing agendas, and it can be tough to sort the wheat from the chaff. For one thing, the vast majority of platforms that qualify as "Catholic" media are owned by the Church, usually in the form of newspapers, radio stations, TV outlets, and websites owned by a given diocese—the *Tablet* in Brooklyn (our partner at Crux), or the *Chicago Catholic*, or *Angelus*, the media platform of the

Archdiocese of Los Angeles (another Crux partner). While these platforms are of tremendous local interest, they generally don't move the needle much in terms of national and international Catholic conversation.

Here I'm not going to try to answer the "What's best?" question, because that's in the eye of the beholder, and, in any event, I have an obvious personal bias as the owner and editor in chief of one of those outlets. Instead, I'll mostly focus on the "Who's most important?" question, since that's more a matter of objective reader or viewer data coupled with the experience of moving in Church circles for a quarter-century.

To begin with the American scene, FreshySites, a US-based web design agency, has identified the most popular Catholic sites in 2022, based on metrics regarding their popularity on social media platforms such as Facebook and Twitter. The list gives the Top 20 Catholic sites, but considering only those that either report news or comment on it, we're left with a Top 14:

1. Catholic News Agency (CNA)
2. Catholic News Service (CNS)
3. EWTN News
4. *National Catholic Register*
5. *National Catholic Reporter*
6. ZENIT
7. Crux
8. *America*
9. *Catholic Herald*

10. *Fr. Z's Blog*
11. Crisis Magazine
12. Catholic World Report (CWR)
13. OnePeterFive
14. Catholic World News (CWN)

As a preliminary observation, it's interesting that fourteen of the twenty most-followed and most-talked about Catholic sites in America are news sites, which suggests an intense interest in news content among those Catholic insiders who spend considerable time on the internet. For whatever it's worth, most of these outlets commonly would be seen as "conservative," while only two, the *National Catholic Reporter* and *America*, are widely seen as falling into the category of "liberal," which probably isn't all that surprising given the data we noted above about the rapid aging of the American population combined with the political trends of older Americans and their disproportionate tendency to consume news content.

It's also worth noting that only one of these sites is truly a personal blog, while the rest are operated by more or less conventional news organizations, which suggests that those outlets are still doing relatively well despite the rise of social media and other alternative media sources. In addition, most of these sites belong to well-established news platforms rather than new start-ups, though OnePeterFive and Crux were launched in 2014.

Given the notorious difficulty of accurately mea-suring exactly how many people are consuming a particular website, due to vast differences in algorithms behind how traffic is assessed and so on, let's consider the breakdown of another widely used internet resource called Feedspot, which is a service for aggregating one's chosen online feeds and collecting them in place. Based on traffic, social media followers, domain authority, and freshness, Feedspot ranks the top Catholic news sites as follows:

1. Catholic News Agency (CNA)
2. *National Catholic Register*
3. EWTN News
4. Catholic News Service (CNS)
5. *National Catholic Reporter*
6. Crux
7. ZENIT
8. *Catholic Herald*
9. *America*
10. *Fr. Z's Blog*
11. Catholic World News (CWN)
12. Crisis Magazine
13. OnePeterFive
14. Catholic World Report (CWR)

Obviously, it's the same cast of characters, with only the relative standings of individual sites varying slightly from list to list. The same observations about the dominance of conservative sites and the relatively strong performance of traditional media outlets applies to the Feedspot countdown as well.

Feedspot's countdown also includes sites in English outside the United States. The top nine English-language Catholic news sites outside the US, according to these rankings, are the following:

1. *The Catholic Register*, Toronto, Canada
2. *The Catholic Weekly*, Sydney, Australia
3. LiCAS News, Manila, Philippines
4. Catholic Digest, London, UK
5. Indian Catholic Matters, Bengaluru, India
6. CathNews, Wellington, New Zealand
7. *NZ Catholic*, Auckland, New Zealand
8. Catholic Insight, Toronto, Canada
9. Catholic News, Kildare, Ireland

Comparing the international English-language list to the domestic, two things stand out. First, these international sites are much less ideologically defined than the American ones. With most of the nine sites listed above, it would be difficult to identify a clear political orientation, but to the extent it's possible, they would range from what Europeans would call "center-left" to "center-right," with the key word probably being "center." Second, and in this case more like the American countdown, most of these sites are also attached to well-established Catholic media operations, as opposed to one-person operations and new start-ups.

In these lists, I've included just the Catholic news sites and omitted every other site that is not primarily a news agency (e.g., Catholic Match, Life Teen, and Church Life Journal). Interestingly, if we look at the overall countdown of all Catholic websites, six of the top ten sites on the FreshySites rundown are news platforms, and they are eight of the top ten on Feedspot. What that appears to suggest is that although most Catholics don't consume Catholic news on a regular basis, those who do consume it fairly intensely.

I should also add that some American Catholics get a good deal of their Church news from sources that are outside the United States and the English-speaking world but offer content in English. *La Croix*, for example, a daily Catholic paper published in France, also operates La Croix International, a platform for Catholic news and commentary that features the work of Robert Mickens, a veteran Vatican-watcher who worked for thirteen years in Vatican Radio and thus brings a deep insider's touch, as well as contributions by Massimo Faggioli, a theologian at Villanova well known for commentary on Church affairs.

Finally, it's important to note that much ground-breaking coverage of the Catholic Church and the Vatican in the English language doesn't come from specifically Catholic platforms, but rather from the mainstream secular press. On the Vatican beat, for example, both Philip Pullella of Reuters and Nicole Winfield of the Associated Press are well-established figures who have developed a deep expertise over time and whose reporting often breaks open stories that the Catholic press follows. Journalists such as Delia Gallagher of CNN, Courtney Walsh of Fox, Francis X. Rocca at the *Wall Street Journal*, and many others also provide sophisticated and well-informed reporting on the Vatican. Undoubtedly, their work reaches much larger audiences than those of us in the specialized Catholic universe, and it shapes the imagination of a much larger cross-section of media consumers.

ESTABLISHMENT AND ANTI-ESTABLISHMENT CATHOLIC MEDIA

As a rule of thumb, liberal Catholics discontent with the establishment in the Church generally just walk away, while conservatives tend to stand and fight. We've seen that phenomenon in the realm of education, for example, where conservatives who believe their local Catholic schools have been corrupted by secularism or are too soft on the faith have either created their own independent schools or become part of a burgeoning Catholic homeschooling movement. The same thing applies at the university level, where the foundations of Thomas Aquinas College in 1971, Christendom College in 1977, and Ave Maria College (now Ave Maria University) in 1998 were, to some extent, referenda on the perceived direction of Catholic higher education in America following Vatican II. In other cases, conservatives may reorient preexisting institutions, as was the case for the Franciscan University of Steubenville in Ohio under the late Fr. Michael Scanlan.

Perhaps nowhere is this tendency as marked, however, as in the Catholic media. Many of today's most influential Catholic media outlets were born, to some extent, out of frustration that established Catholic media were either too institutional to be forthright in confronting leadership failures or too compromised by secular liberalism to defend the faith adequately when it runs afoul of conventional secular wisdom. During the early 1980s, for instance, Mother Angelica's main competitor in building a national Catholic television platform was the National Catholic Telecommunications Network, sponsored by the US Catholic bishops. The bishops poured $30 million into the project before being compelled to admit defeat, and one of the reasons EWTN prevailed is because their largely conservative fans and donors frankly trusted Mother Angelica more than the bishops to tell it like it is. (Her legendary feistiness, having once told a left-leaning bishop that he could "go put his head in the back toilet," was all part of the appeal.) The Catholic News Agency, owned by EWTN, was likewise founded in part as a competitor to the Catholic News Service, the official outlet of the US bishops until 2022, in part due to a diagnosis that CNS was too shackled to the institution and too liberal to be fair to conservative viewpoints.

The animus between EWTN and more liberal elements in the Catholic Church arguably reached a crescendo in 2021, when Pope Francis during an airborne news conference said that media outlets that attack his papacy are doing "the work of the devil," referring in particular to "a large Catholic television channel that has no hesitation in continually speaking ill of the pope." It was widely taken as a reference to EWTN, prompting a predictable cycle of glee on the Catholic left and umbrage on the right.

Yet under the law that "once a revolution begins, you can't control where it ends," in recent years there's been a notable increase in both formal Catholic news platforms and informal blogs and social media offerings that stand to the right of even conservative outlets such as EWTN, the *National Catholic Register*, and *First Things*. Many would call these new initiatives "alt-right," though since that term was originally coined in the context of white nationalist media in the United States and therefore carries racist connotations, here I'll refer to these new Catholic operations as "hard-right." Because many of them also express fondness for the older Latin Mass and other traditional forms of liturgical expression, I'll also use the term "traditionalist." It's possible to be one without the other, though in general the two instincts overlap.

Some of these platforms attract large followings online. According to Alexa traffic rankings as of February 2022, Church Militant, for example, draws roughly the same number of internet users as the Catholic News Agency, the *National Catholic Reporter*, and Crux. Others are considerably smaller in terms of traffic, but they often have an outsized influence by virtue of being picked up and cited by more mainstream media and on social media platforms when breaking news occurs. Another feature is their contentious relationship with Church authorities, in some cases leading to individual bishops or bishops' conferences publicly stating these platforms are not recognized as "Catholic."

Another distinguishing feature of the hard-right/ traditionalist constellation in the Catholic media is its aggressiveness, often shading off into pointed personal attacks. To take just one randomly chosen example, in February 2022, the influential blogger Fr. Z posted an entry about a priest in Chicago who closes his Masses with a rock-style guitar blessing, referring to the priest as "Fr. Jackass" and going on to suggest that the "real goal" of such departures from traditional liturgical practice is "non-celibate (non-continent) homosexual clergy."

The "Fr. Jackass" example also points to another characteristic of the hard-right/traditionalist media, which is a conscious disregard of established principles of journalistic practice. If a reporter for the *New York Times*, or *Figaro*, or the BBC wanted to publicly identify a specific priest with a push for openly gay and sexually active clergy, that reporter would be obligated to at least make an attempt to contact the priest and give him the opportunity to confirm or deny. In this case, there's no indication from the blog entry that any such attempt was made. In fairness, the blog at that point was suggesting that Catholics who attack the traditional liturgy have such an agenda, without explicitly saying that this includes the guitar-playing priest, but the implication nevertheless seemed clear.

Critics of the hard-right and traditionalist Catholic media, who include many strong conservatives, believe all this adds up to willing participation in the culture of contempt. Their admirers, on the other hand, are generally willing to forgive a certain sloppiness in reporting and sometimes overheated rhetoric as the price of having the courage to speak truth to power.

Based partly on traffic reports and partly on subjective impressions of influence, here's a run of nine of the most important Catholic hard-right/traditionalist media platforms.

- **Church Militant:** In most ways, Church Militant is the paradigmatic hard-right Catholic media platform, and it would be what most Catholics have in mind when they use such terms. Based in Michigan, Church Militant was founded by Michael Voris, a former secular radio and television personality, as the world's first entirely online Catholic TV network. Its original name was Real Catholic TV, but Voris changed it in 2012 after the Archdiocese of Detroit notified the network that "it does not regard them as being authorized to use the word 'Catholic' to identify or promote their public activities." Its centerpiece program is "The Vortex," Voris' evening news and commentary show, and it has an annual budget of about $2.8 million. Church Militant is often compared to Breitbart, the secular news agency founded by Steve Bannon, and the network tends to be highly supportive of former President Donald Trump.

- **LifeSite News:** The most widely read hard-right/traditionalist Catholic news platform, LifeSite News posts traffic numbers that, again according to Alexa rankings, place it well ahead of more established Catholic media outlets such as the *National Catholic Reporter* or the Catholic News Agency. It was founded in Canada in 1997 as a platform for pro-life voices, based on a conviction that the mainstream secular media is against the pro-life position. It has since become a general interest news site with a hard-right editorial orientation. LifeSite's Twitter and Facebook accounts have been temporarily suspended at least four times since 2018, in two cases for use of alleged hate speech with regard to transgendered individuals and once for allegedly spreading misinformation about the COVID-19 pandemic.
- **OnePeterFive:** Founded by Catholic journalist and essayist Steve Skojec, OnePeterFive is legally based in Scottsdale, Arizona, with a workforce of thirty and a reported budget of $5 million.

OnePeterFive often functions as a launching pad from which Catholic stories enter the mainstream media. In 2017, a writer on the site published a report of a meeting between Pope Francis and the former head of the Vatican's doctrinal department, German Cardinal Gerhard Müller, that described an acrimonious exchange in which Francis fired Müller for holding conservative positions on issues such as woman deacons, priestly celibacy, and giving communion to Catholics who divorce and remarry outside the Church. Müller later denied that account, as did the Vatican's spokesperson at the time, American journalist Greg Burke.

- *Fr. Z's Blog*: Operated by Fr. John Zuhlsdorf, an American priest formerly of the Diocese of Madison in Wisconsin and now incardinated in the Diocese of Velletri-Segni in Italy, *Fr. Z's Blog* is among the most popular Catholic entries in the blogosphere. It was formerly known as *What Does the Prayer Really Say?*, reflecting a concern for defense of traditional Catholic liturgy. Yet Zuhlsdorf comments on a wide variety of other topics, and in January 2021, controversy erupted when he livestreamed a video of himself performing an exorcism against participants in the United States Electoral College Vote Count. It was later announced that Zuhlsdorf would no longer have permission to conduct ministries in the Diocese of Madison.

- ***Rorate Caeli:*** Rorate Caeli is a traditionalist blog that provides news and commentary on Catholic affairs. It began operations in 2005, and its founder and chief contributor is anonymous, presenting himself under the epithet "New Catholic" and describing himself as a Catholic convert and layman. It also hosts contributions from clergy, some identified by name and some anonymous. In traditionalist/Catholic circles, *Rorate Caeli* is considered a leading point of reference, especially on liturgical matters.

- **Novus Ordo Watch:** The thrust of Novus Ordo Watch, a leading sedevacantist site, can be gleaned from the motto on its homepage, which reads, "Unmasking the modernist Vatican II church." Legally based in Springdale, Ohio, a suburb of Cincinnati, Novus Ordo Watch is a project of Interregnum Foundation, which was first assigned nonprofit status in 2016. Its owner is Mario Derksen, a forty-one-year-old German-born revert to Catholicism who embraced the traditionalist cause and its rejection of the post–Vatican II Mass.

- **Taylor Marshall:** A former priest in the Episcopalian Church of the United States, Marshall is a 2006 convert to Catholicism who's gone on to become an influential voice in traditionalist and anti-establishment Catholic circles. In 2019, he published *Infiltration: The Plot to Destroy the Church from Within*, a book arguing that the Catholic Church's hierarchy has been subverted in recent decades to promote Masonic aims. During the 2019 Synod of Bishops on the Amazon, Marshall funded a trip to Rome by a traditionalist named Alexander Tschugguel, who stole an icon of the Pachamama, an indigenous Amazon fertility figure, from a Roman church and tossed it into the Tiber River, with Marshall later publicizing the act by uploading video of it. Marshall boasts 400,000 subscribers on YouTube, and his social media comments have been retweeted, among others, by former President Donald Trump.

- **Gloria.tv:** Described as an internet-based Catholic video sharing and news site, Gloria.tv was founded in Switzerland in 2005 and based for a time in Moldova, but in 2017 it moved its legal registration to Dover, Delaware. The site was founded by a Swiss priest named Fr. Reto Nay, although Nay has not been listed on the site since 2014 after he was removed from office by the bishop of the Swiss diocese of Chur over publishing comments seen as anti-Semitic. The leading German news magazine *Die Spiegel* has described Gloria.tv as "a kind of YouTube for Catholic radicals."

- **InfoVaticana** (Spanish): Based in Spain, Info-Vaticana is the leading hard-right/traditionalist media platform in the Spanish language. It began operations in 2013 and began publishing in Italian in 2015. In addition to its own staff-generated content, InfoVaticana also hosts blogs by several traditionalist commentators, most of whom tend to be sharply critical of Pope Francis. In 2017, the Vatican asked that InfoVaticana transfer its domain name to the Holy See and refrain from using images that might suggest any connection to official Vatican communications channels, prompting the site's founder, Gabriel Ariza, to respond that the Vatican was engaged in a "political witch hunt" and that "they just want to shut us down."

By way of general observations, it's striking that only two of the platforms, LifeSite News and *Fr. Z's Blog*, were founded before the year 2000, and the majority date to no earlier than 2005. The hard-right/traditionalist Catholic media is thus a relatively recent phenomenon. It's also noteworthy that the hard-right/traditionalist Catholic media tends to spotlight anonymous content, and, in some cases, even the ownership and editorial control of these platforms is disguised. A third point is that these platforms often explicitly attack established Catholic media; InfoVaticana, for example, has campaigned against Religión Digital, describing it as a website "that harbors all kinds of blasphemies while being financed by the church" and a "shredder of everything that today remains Catholic, despicable mis-representers of the truth . . . outright liars."

While it's often said that these media platforms appeal to only a small minority of Catholics, that shouldn't obscure the significance of their accomplishment. Within a short arc of time, many of these platforms have built audiences comparable to, or exceeding, mainstream outlets, and they often launch stories into orbit, compelling mainstream platforms to follow their lead. In a word, they're a force with which Catholic media today must reckon.

BEYOND ENGLISH

It's important to have begun this survey among English-language news platforms, given that English is by far the most widely used language on the internet and that we live in an age in which even long-established print publications draw most of their readership online. The *New York Times*, for example, now has 8.4 million total subscriptions, of which 7.6 million are digital and only 795,000 are print. The dominance of English on the internet, especially among the most-visited sites, is well established. According to W3Techs, a provider of web technology surveys, if we consider the top 10 million websites on the internet as of 2021, 63.4 percent were in English. Similarly, of the top 250 YouTube channels, 66 percent were in English. Granted, Chinese is almost level with English as the native language of today's internet users, but the vast majority of Chinese speakers spend most of their time online accessing English-language content. Wikipedia reports that among its visitors each day, 257 million access pages in English, with the next most-used language, Japanese, drawing just 37 million.

In terms of the global Catholic scene, by far the highest traffic levels belong to sites in English, and most of those are American. That said, it's nevertheless key to cast our nets wider, outside the United States and outside the English language, because citing traffic numbers is not the only way of answering the question of which Catholic news sites are most important.

As I said in the introduction, we have to start with Italian. If you go onto the official Vatican website, you'll find content offered in nine languages, which more or less represent its official working languages: Italian, French, Spanish, Portuguese, English, German, Arabic, Mandarin Chinese, and Latin. Of that set, Italian is by far the least-spoken language these days apart from Latin. Mandarin, Spanish, and English are, respectively, the three most-spoken languages in the world; Portuguese is in sixth place, and French, German, and Arabic are all in the top twenty. In one sense, you might think we could almost afford to ignore Italian and focus more on other languages, perhaps especially Spanish, which is the native tongue of almost half of the 1.36 billion Catholics in the world.

While we will consider Spanish in a moment, Italian nevertheless claims a pride of place in any Catholic survey. While Italian may not be a top finisher among the most-spoken languages overall, it certainly is among the languages most frequently spoken by Catholic bishops around the world. If we were to conduct a poll of bishops to find their most common second language, there's little doubt Italian would be near the top of the list. A strong share of the world's episcopacy either studied in Rome or lived and worked there for some stretch of time. Some may have been here working in a Vatican department, some working for another Catholic institution, some serving on the leadership teams of their religious orders.

Consider five of the most important prelates in the American Church as of this writing: Cardinal Joseph Tobin of Newark served in Rome for thirteen years as the superior of his order, the Redemptorists; Cardinal Timothy Dolan of New York spent 1994 to 2001 in Rome as the rector of the Pontifical North American College (NAC), the residence for American seminarians in the Eternal City; Cardinal Wilton Gregory of Washington, DC, studied in Rome from 1976 to 1980, earning a doctorate in liturgy from the Benedictine-run Pontifical Institute of Sant'Anselmo; Cardinal Blase Cupich of Chicago lived at the NAC from 1971 to 1975, earning a master's degree in theology from the Jesuit-run

Gregorian University; and Cardinal Daniel DiNardo not only lived at the NAC and earned degrees from both the Gregorian and the Augustinian Patristic Institute, but later served from 1984 to 1990 on the staff of the Vatican's ultra-important Congregation for Bishops.

Despite the evident differences among these five senior figures, one thing they all have in common is varying degrees of Roman seasoning. The same point could be made about virtually any Catholic nation in the world: among its crop of bishops, especially those who rise through the system and end up in the most influential positions, a strong share is likely to have had Roman experience at some point in their careers.

While ordinary Catholics around the world who haven't had much experience of Rome and don't read Italian obviously aren't consuming much Catholic news produced in Italian, bishops do. The same point could be made about other movers and shakers in the Church, including the heads of Catholic movements, the superiors of religious orders, and the presidents and CEOs of major Catholic institutions. Moreover, given the widely held assumption that the Italians are more wired into the Vatican than other language groups, these movers and shakers are probably inclined to spend more time consulting Italian news platforms and to take what they find seriously.

In addition, there's another class of insider Catholics who also take the Italian press extremely seriously: journalists specialized on the Catholic beat, most of whom, at one stage or another, will spend a stretch in Rome seeing the Vatican up close and personal. Frankly, if you're interested in how the press actually works, it's worth it to learn some Italian just to watch how many stories make it into English, Spanish, and other languages after starting out in Italian. Here's a true story: When I first arrived in Rome, I met a veteran correspondent for a major secular paper outside the US. He was well known for writing what would be known today as "clickbait" stories, like "Priest's girlfriend has baby" or "Swiss Guard linked to sex sting." I once ran into him at Rome's Foreign Press Club, and I asked his secret. "I get in here around 10:00 in the morning, and I spread the Italian papers out in front of me," he said. "I look for the craziest stuff, maybe make a couple phone calls to freshen it up, and then file. Most days I'm done by 1:00 p.m. and on my way to a long boozy lunch." Naturally, he was exaggerating a bit for comic effect, and most foreign reporters on the Rome beat don't roll that way. Still, I do sometimes wonder what news agencies in English, Spanish, etc. based in Rome would do if the entire Italian press shut down for a day. It would not be a day for a bumper crop of Catholic news around the world, I can tell you that. (There are occasionally journalist strikes in Italy, by the way, but like most things here, the whole thing generally is a bit chaotic and disunified, and inevitably some outlets are still operating.)

Finally, here's another reason why people in the know in the Church tend to follow the Italian scene: whether you think it should matter or not, Vatican personnel take it seriously, and it therefore exercises an outsized impact of their sense of what's going on. One of the reasons the Vatican was painfully slow to respond to the clerical sexual abuse scandals in the United States in 2002–2003, for example, was because the Italian press has not given the same attention to the abuse crisis in the Church as the press in most other Western cultures, and, to the extent it was covered back in 2002–2003, it was mostly presented as a media story about the overreaction of the American press.

I was once present when a senior Vatican official was asked why they pay so much attention to, say, *Il Messaggero*, a local newspaper in Rome with a circulation of about 127,000, as opposed to, say, the BBC, with over a billion monthly visits to its website, or the *New York Times*, which, as we've seen, has over eight million subscribers, or *Le Monde*, more or less the paper of record in France and across the French-speaking world. "Ma Il Messaggero è lì," he replied. "Si può toccarlo. . . . Gli altri sono lontani." ("But Il Messaggero is right here. You can touch it. . . . These others are far away.")

For all these reasons, then, it's important to bring Italy into view. Here's a list of the ten most important news sites for matters regarding the Catholic Church in Italian, measured both by objective data such as traffic and also anecdotal experience about how often a particular platform is cited by influential Catholic figures in informal conversation. You'll note as well that several of these outlets aren't Catholic but secular news organizations. That's because the distinction in Italy is always fuzzy, and anyway, even the most ardently anti-clerical and atheistic news platforms cover the Church on a regular basis because it's such a dominant cultural force in the country.

Let's begin with the top five official sources of Catholic news in Italy, in order of readership and importance.

1. Vatican News, the official news site of the Holy See
2. *Avvenire*, the official newspaper of the Italian bishops
3. *L'Osservatore Romano*, the official newspaper of the Holy See
4. *La Civiltà Cattolica*, a Jesuit-edited journal that enjoys semi-official Vatican status because it's read by the Secretariat of State before publication
5. Vatican Radio, the site of the Vatican's official radio service

Vatican News was launched in 2017 as the first fruit of Pope Francis' sweeping reorganization of the communications operation, the heart of which was the creation of a new "Secretariat of Communications" to bring together what previously had been a welter of more or less autonomous operations. The idea was to save money by consolidating resources, while at the same time presenting a more unified and coordinated message. Most observers would say five years later that it hasn't fully accomplished either aim; communications, especially Vatican Radio, is still a major drain on the annual budget, and it doesn't seem notably more coordinated either. For one thing, Vatican News and the Vatican Press Office sometimes don't seem to have their act together. Even though it's the role of the press office to share important news with accredited journalists before it breaks, under embargo, so the press corps can be ready when the time comes, often important tidbits will appear on Vatican News before the press office has said a word to anybody.

Among these five, *Avvenire* may be the most respected, in the sense that its coverage tends to be the closest thing to independent journalism that an official news outlet can provide. It also tends to be the most thorough and comprehensive, covering not only a wide range of specifically Catholic news but also commenting on the Italian political and cultural scene as well as international affairs, such the George Floyd protests in the United States and the Capitol riots. If you want a semi-official soundbite on Italy's debate over gay marriage, for example, or assisted suicide, *Avvenire* is often your best resource, and it also comes in handy for hunting Roman reactions to American news.

As for *Civiltà Cattolica*, traditionally most people likely would have ranked it as the least consequential of these five outlets. It's an academic journal at heart and often veers into eggheaded territory like "Imagining a conversation between Wittgenstein and Suarez" or "The hermeneutical roots of Paul Claudel's poetry." However, in the Pope Francis era, it has become an increasingly important source of insight, in part because it's run by the pope's fellow Jesuits, but mostly because its editor, Jesuit Fr. Antonio Spadaro, is among the pontiff's closest advisors and arguably—though more informally than Francis' official spokesman, Italian layman Matteo Bruni—a voice on behalf of the pope.

In terms of nonofficial Catholic news sites in Italy, based upon traffic numbers and how often they're cited in other media, the following are among the most influential. Given that the rankings are inexact, I'm listing them in alphabetical order.

- **AsiaNews:** Operated by the Pontifical Institute for Foreign Missions, a group of priests and laity devoted to missionary work, AsiaNews was originally launched in Italian and now offers content in other languages. As the name implies, it largely covers Catholic news out of Asia, and people tend to follow it especially for its coverage of China and Vatican-China affairs.

- *Famiglia Cristiana*: One of the highest-circulation weekly magazines in Italy, *Famiglia Cristiana* is published by the Society of St. Paul, or "Paulines," a religious order devoted to mass communications founded in Italy in 1914. The magazine mostly covers Italian politics, pop culture, fashion, and domestic topics, but it does occasionally dip into Catholic news too.

- *Jesus*: Specifically focused on Catholic news and culture, *Jesus* was also launched by the Paulines, although it's now an autonomous platform. It tends to be a place not for breaking news but for deep dives into matters of Catholic interest. Coverage focuses not just on the Catholic Church but on other major faith traditions as well, in the spirit of interfaith dialogue associated with the Second Vatican Council.

- **Korazym:** Initially founded as a follow-up to the 2002 World Youth Day in Toronto, Korazym has come to be an independent news and commentary site on Catholic affairs. Its director is Vik van Brantegem, a Dutch Belgian who served as an aide and media liaison for papal trips in the Vatican Press Office under St. John Paul II.

- **La Nuova Bussola Quotidiana:** Founded in 2012 by Italian journalist Riccardo Cascioli, La Nuova Bussola is an independent digital platform offering news and opinion on Catholic affairs. Beginning in December 2019, the platform has also offered material in English and Spanish.

- **Radio Maria:** Founded in 1982 in the country's north by a priest named Fr. Marco Galbiati, Radio Maria is now Italy's largest independent Catholic radio provider. It's funded in part by listener contributions and in part by public funding. By statute, all employees of Radio Maria are required to be practicing Catholics and to profess loyalty to Church teaching.

- *Settimo Cielo*: The personal blog of veteran journalist Sandro Magister, who has covered Vatican and Catholic affairs for *L'Espresso*, Italy's most widely read newsmagazine, since 1974. Magister has offered this blog since 2003, and it's also available in English, Spanish, and French, making it one of the most widely read sources of Vatican analysis in the Catholic world.

- **S.I.R.:** Short for *Servizio Informazione Religiosa*, or "Religious Information Service," S.I.R. is more or less the official news agency of the Italian bishops' conference.

- *Il Sismografo*: The blog operated by Luis Badilla, a Chilean who once served as a minister in the government of Chile's leftist President Salvador Allende until he was overthrown by a military coup in 1973. Badilla escaped and fled to Rome, spending many years working in Vatican Radio. *Il Sismografo* collects important articles about the Church and the Vatican from media in various languages and occasionally offers personal commentary.

- *Stilum Curiae*: Another personal blog, this one operated by another veteran Vatican journalist named Marco Tosatti, who wrote for many years for the major Italian daily *La Stampa*. The site is financed by reader contributions, and Tosatti describes his aim as resisting a tendency to what he sees as the press making itself "servile" with respect to the institutions it covers.

- **Vatican Insider:** A project of *La Stampa*, Vatican Insider is a digital platform providing news and analysis of Vatican and Catholic affairs in Italian, English, and Spanish. It reached its high-water mark in terms of influence when it was edited by Andrea Tornielli, a longtime Vatican journalist, before Tornielli was named the Vatican's first-ever Editorial Director by Pope Francis in 2018.

Surveying this list, at least three things stand out compared to the English-speaking world. To begin with, the Italian scene is less dominated by the Catholic right than the United States. Of the eleven sites listed above, five would generally be considered conservative, ranging from moderately to strongly so (Korazym, Nuova Bussola, Radio Maria, *Settimo Cielo*, and *Stilum Curiae*), while four are perceived as leaning to the left to varying degrees (*Famiglia Cristiana*, *Jesus*, *Sismografo*, and Vatican Insider). That leaves two news agencies, AsiaNews and S.I.R., to which it would be difficult to ascribe a particular ideological orientation. Second, there's a stronger presence of relatively new platforms among the top independent Catholic sites in Italy than in the English-speaking world, perhaps in part because established operations in Italy were a bit slower to migrate into the digital realm. Third, it's noteworthy how blogs operated by a lone individual can hold their own against platforms with much deeper pockets. It illustrates one of the eternal truths of the media business: you can pour all the money you want into hardware and delivery systems, but if you don't have content people want, all those resources don't really matter. Content, in other words, is king.

Finally, we also need to briefly look at the secular media scene in Italy, which is unique in the world in that every major daily newspaper here has at least one full-time correspondent assigned to the Catholic and Vatican beat, sometimes more than one, and the same can be said for radio and TV. The national public broadcaster RAI (*Radiotelevisione italiana*) actually has an entire department, the *Struttura Vaticana*, dedicated to Vatican coverage and, among other things, broadcasts of all major papal events and trips. During the Pope John Paul II years and again today under Pope Francis, the Vatican beat is among the most coveted in journalism, seen as occupying a level of importance equivalent to or even greater than covering the prime minister. As a result, Italian Catholics aren't dependent mostly on Catholic media organizations to get their news about the Church. Indeed, when you say "Vatican journalist" (the word here is Vaticanista) to most Italians, they won't think of someone working for a Catholic outfit, but rather of well-known writers and broadcasters for major secular outlets.

On that landscape, the most important mainstream platforms offering Catholic news are as follows.

- **ANSA:** Short for *Agenzia Nazionale Stampa Associata* (Associated National Press Agency), ANSA is the Associated Press of Italy. It has several correspondents who cover the Vatican, but probably its main beat reporter today is Manuela Tulli, a career journalist known for her command of detail.

- *Corriere della Sera*: More or less Italy's *New York Times*, meaning the paper of record, *Corriere* was home for many years to the work of legendary Vatican correspondent Luigi Accattoli. He was so hardwired that once during a Synod of Bishops, other journalists got so frustrated with his daily scoops about the supposedly confidential proceedings that we semi-jokingly proposed that the Vatican ask Accattoli to give the briefings rather than their official mouthpieces. Today the lead Vatican correspondent is Gian Guido Vecchi, a journalist with close ties to the Community of Sant'Egidio.

- *La Repubblica*: Italy's highest-circulation newspaper, *La Repubblica* has a left-leaning editorial orientation. Its Vatican correspondent until recently was Paolo Rodari, who started his career at the leftist *Riformista*, then worked for the neo-conservative *Il Foglio* before joining *Repubblica*.

- ***Il Messaggero*:** Italy's leading paper based in Rome, *Messaggero* for a long stretch featured the work of Orazio Petrosillo, another legendary Vatican reporter known for his encyclopedia-like command of obscure papal trivia. Today its lead Vatican writer is Franca Giansoldati, a veteran of ANSA who, in 2014, became one of the few women to have interviewed a pope.

- ***La Stampa*:** Based in Turin, *La Stampa* is the sponsor of Vatican Insider. Its lead Vatican correspondent today is Domenico Agasso, the grandson of Domenico Agasso Sr., a legendary Italian journalist who covered Pope Paul VI's early overseas trips, including his voyage to the Holy Land. It also features the work of veteran Vatican writer Giacomo Galeazzi, also responsible for *La Stampa*'s desk for investigative journalism.

- **RAI:** As mentioned above, Italy's national broadcaster employs a whole team of journalists specializing in Vatican coverage. Among the better-known figures at RAI today offering Vatican news and analysis are Vania De Luca, Ignazio Ingrao, and Enzo Romeo.

- ***Il Fatto Quotidiano*:** Broadly leftist in outlook, *Il Fatto* was named in honor of a legendary Italian journalist kicked out at the insistence of Berlusconi when he was prime minister. Today it features opinion pieces by Marco Politi, who covered the Vatican for *La Repubblica* from 1993 to 2009 after serving as the paper's foreign correspondent in Moscow.

Like any other small world overpopulated with alpha personalities, Italy's Vatican press corps is renowned for its personal rivalries and animosities, which sometimes erupt in full public view. In 2017, for example, Tornielli, now the Vatican's Editorial Director, crossed swords with Cascioli of La Nuova Bussola, publishing a stinging piece titled "Lies of the Nuova Bussola" after Cascioli had accused him of trying to get German Cardinal Walter Brandmüller to say negative things about American Cardinal Raymond Burke, both of whom were signatories of a set of critical questions to Pope Francis about his cautious opening of Communion to Catholics who divorce and remarry outside the Church. It was, Tornielli wrote, "a poisonous and false accusation, which reveals the hearts and describes well the level reached by those who teach journalism and doctrine to everyone every day, believing themselves to be a new Holy Office." Cascioli fired back, "When choosing the profession of a sniper, one must be aware it's a dangerous profession."

Such spats are in one sense ideological, in that prior to his Vatican appointment in December 2018, Tornielli was widely seen as the leading defender of Pope Francis in Italian Catholic media—so much so that one conservative Italian Vatican writer, Giuseppe

Rusconi, derisively labeled Tornielli the pope's *turiferario maggiore*, meaning his main incense-bearer. Cascioli, meanwhile, is seen as ferociously anti-Francis; around the same time his contretemps with Tornielli broke out, Cascioli was also in hot water for publicly defending a series of anti-Francis posters in Rome accusing him of being a dictator. Yet they're also personal, since, as is often the case, Tornielli and Cascioli are also former colleagues who once worked together, as Tornielli for a brief period served as the director of the platform that preceded La Nuova Bussola, where Cascioli was on staff.

In sum, Italy tends to be where a lion's share of the action is in terms of media coverage of the Catholic Church, both in the specialized Catholic press and in the mainstream secular media. In truth, it can often be difficult here to tell the difference between the two, and frankly, you could argue that there really isn't much difference.

THE SPANISH WORLD

As of early 2021, roughly 48 percent of the world's 1.36 billion Catholics lived in Latin America, meaning around six hundred million people. Add to that the thirty million Catholics in Spain, and Spanish is easily the most common native language in the Church. Those numbers mean that developments in Spanish-language Catholicism matter to the entire Church, especially, of course, in the era of history's first Latin American pope.

I don't speak Spanish, nor do I know the world of Latin American Catholicism especially well beyond occasional brief trips over the years, usually in the company of a pope—and believe me when I say, when you travel with a pope you move in a bubble, so it's not quite the best way to encounter the realities on the ground. Therefore, I turned to my Crux colleague Inés San Martín—who's a native Argentinian and who, beyond her reporting on the Vatican, also provides terrific regular coverage of the Latin American scene—for an assist. She, in turn, carried out an informal survey among either consumers or producers of Catholic news in Spanish and put together a list of the most influential destinations.

In terms of general observations, San Martín notes that "Spanish speakers are not as avid religion news consumers as English speakers. Those who do [follow Church news] are arguably as extremist and divided as English speakers. Conservatives, particularly traditionalists, are reading more these days because they love to complain and rant against whatever the pope said last that they don't like." She also noted that, with a few exceptions, most of these news outlets are based in Spain rather than Latin America, meaning that Spanish-language Catholic media coverage often has a more European orientation.

That said, here's her list of the most important Catholic news platforms in Spanish:

- **ACI Prensa:** Founded in Lima, Peru, in 1980, ACI Prensa is a daily Catholic news agency. Since 1987 its director has been Alejandro Bermúdez Rosell, who also launched and directs the Catholic News Agency in the US. Since 2014, both ACI Prensa and CNA have been part of the EWTN platform.

- **COPE:** Owned by the Spanish bishops' conference, COPE is the second most popular radio network in the country. Originally created to broadcast religious content, it's evolved into a general interest radio platform, although its news operation still gives special attention to Church affairs. A former Rome correspondent for COPE, Paloma García Ovejero, served as the deputy spokesperson for the Vatican from 2016 to 2018.

- **EFE:** Spain's version of the Associated Press, EFE is the world's fourth largest wire service. It provides regular coverage of the Vatican and Church affairs that is often picked up not only in Spain but across Latin America.

- **InfoVaticana:** Founded in 2013, InfoVaticana describes itself as "filling a gap in rigorous analysis of what happens in the Church." It's known for emphasizing doctrinal orthodoxy and criticism of the Francis papacy and has even been sued by the Vatican for copyright infringement for using the word "Vatican" and employing Vatican symbols.

- **Rome Reports:** Founded by a group of Spanish journalists and outlets, Rome Reports is an international TV news agency based in Rome that provides coverage of the pope and the Vatican, used largely by television platforms that can't afford their own Rome presence. Though its center of gravity is in the Spanish-speaking world, it offers content in English as well.
- **Vatican News (in Spanish):** This is the Spanish version of the Vatican's official news platform described above.
- **Vida Nueva Digital:** Founded in Spain in 1958, *Vida Nueva* is a weekly print publication that also operates an active daily website offering news and commentary on Catholic affairs. Its director is José Beltrán, its Vatican correspondent is Dario Menor, and the platform's editorial line is seen as more or less centrist.
- **Religión Digital:** Founded in 2000 by veteran Spanish Catholic journalist José Manuel Vidal, Religión Digital claims to be the most-read source of Catholic news in Spanish with five million visitors a month. It operates a special web page, "Pro Francisco," to demonstrate its explicit support for the reforming agenda of Pope Francis.
- **Aleteia:** Launched in 2011, Aleteia was designed from the beginning to be a global Catholic platform, offering content in six languages: Spanish, Italian, English, French, Portuguese, and Arabic.

Its director is Jesús Colina, who formerly headed the ZENIT news agency and who served as a consultant for the Pontifical Council for Social Communications under Pope Benedict XVI.

- **Catholic.net:** A multimedia platform, Catholic.net is analogous to EWTN but with a somewhat less hard-edge news focus, concentrating more on matters of Catholic spirituality and faith development.

Of those ten outlets, five would be seen as basically conservative, though in varying ways and to varying degrees, while at least three are fairly clearly on the left. As mentioned above, Vida Nueva would be seen as more moderate—San Martín actually describes it as the closest thing in Spanish to what Crux tries to do in English—while Vatican News is the state media channel of the Vatican. It's also interesting that most of the principal Spanish Catholic news sites are relatively new, which again suggests a relative slowness of traditional media organizations to plant their flags online.

Beyond outlets that are specifically Catholic, there are also several mainstream news organizations in the Spanish-speaking world that provide content from well-respected reporters and journalists covering the Vatican and the Catholic Church. In Mexico, for example, probably the most influential journalist covering the Vatican is Valentina Alazraki, who was on the papal plane for 100 of Pope John Paul II's 104 foreign trips and who is today considered the co-dean of the Vatican Press Corps along with Pullella from Reuters. Elisabetta Piqué, who writes from Rome for the Argentine daily *La Nación*, is a veteran war correspondent who's also very close to Pope Francis and published a biography in 2013 that became the basis for the film *Francis: Pray for Me*. Her husband, Gerard O'Connell, is the Vatican correspondent for *America* magazine in the US.

FRENCH AND GERMAN

While English, Italian, and Spanish are the dominant languages for Catholic media around the world, it's also important to include at least a brief consideration of the most important platforms in both French and German, since both are churches with considerable resources and countries with a very active press culture.

Here's a rundown of ten prominent German and French Catholic news providers.

- **Katholische Nachrichten-Agentur (KNA):** Reckoned to be the largest and most widely read Catholic news agency in Europe, KNA was founded in 1952 under the aegis of the German bishops' conference, and to this day the bishops remain by far the largest shareholders in the agency's parent company. Its current editor in chief is Ludwig Ring-Eifel, who formerly served as KNA's Vatican correspondent.

- **Deutsche Welle:** Germany's state-owned public broadcast service, Deutsche Welle does not provide regular coverage of Catholic affairs. Yet because of the size of its overall audience, when Deutsche Welle does dip into Catholic coverage, it tends to have an outsized impact.

- *Die Tagespost*: Founded in 1948 and based in Würzburg, *Die Tagespost* is an independent weekly newspaper and online platform covering the Catholic Church that's generally perceived as conservative; it was the leading case in point when the president of the powerful Central Committee of German Catholics warned in 2019 of growing "right-wing influences" on German parishes.

- **Katholisches.info:** An independent online media platform that delivers Catholic news and opinion, usually from a fairly conservative point of view. It broke the story, for instance, of an Augsburg-based publisher belonging to the German bishops involved in the porn trade, and it was also among the first to surface a controversy from Limburg regarding certificates issued by Catholic counseling centers that one conservative bishop called a "license to kill."

- **kath.net:** An independent online platform for Catholic news and commentary that's based in Austria, kath.net is supported by advertising and contributions from Catholic organizations such as Aid to the Church in Need. It also operates a

YouTube channel. Munich-based priest Fr. Andreas Wollbold has described kath.net as having "a clearly conservative orientation."

- *La Croix*: First published in 1880, *La Croix* is a daily newspaper that achieved early fame by accusing Alfred Dreyfus of treason and stirring up anti-Semitism in French public opinion. Over time it's reinvented itself as a general-interest newspaper and today is the mostly widely read Catholic publication in France. As noted above, it also sponsors a specifically Catholic digital platform with a wide following both in French and in English.

- **I.Media:** Founded in the early 1990s by a veteran Rome-based French reporter named Jean-Marie Guénois, I.Media is a digital news agency covering the Vatican whose reporting is picked up by major French outlets such as *Le Figaro* and Agence France-Presse. It's a subscription-based service and provides content to both secular and Catholic media outlets. Given the size of its reporting presence in Rome, I.Media is among the more influential Catholic media platforms in French.

- **KTO:** Founded in 1999 under the late Cardinal Jean-Marie Lustiger, KTO is the principal Catholic television service in French, and, although legally independent, it maintains ties with the French bishops' conference. It broadcasts 24/7 both via cable and satellite carriers and also on-line, and it's available in most French-speaking countries.

- *Le Pèlerin*: First published as a weekly newspaper by the Assumptionist Fathers in 1877, *Pèlerin* is owned by Bayard Press along with *La Croix* and *Notre Temps* and is the most widely circulated Catholic weekly in France. Alongside its regular news coverage, *Pèlerin* also published special editions on themes such as pilgrimage and France's Catholic cultural heritage. It doesn't ask readers to pay for access to content and also posts material on Facebook. Editorially, it's generally seen as center-left and broadly enthusiastic about the Francis papacy.

- *Famille chrétienne*: A weekly Catholic news magazine, *Famille chrétienne* has been published in France since 1978. It began life as a sister publication of *Famiglia Cristiana* in Italy, but since 1992 it's been merged with the French media company Média-Participations, which also owns I.Media. Generally speaking, it's seen as leaning to the right on matters of both ecclesiastical and secular politics.

AFRICA AND ASIA

Catholic media tends to be fairly rudimentary in much of the developing world. Often, Catholic radio and

TV outlets do little more than broadcast liturgies and spiritual programming, and whatever news content they may offer is often taken from platforms in the first world. However, both Africa and Asia also feature a handful of news platforms that generate original content and have an impact on Catholic conversation in those regions. The following are what many observers would regard as the five most significant.

- **UCAN:** The Union of Catholic Asian News is a news agency launched in Hong Kong in 1979. Content is provided in English as well as in Chinese, Indonesian, South Korean, and Vietnamese. Internal wrangles in 2019 threatened to see UCAN effectively divide into two separate operations, but it remains the largest Catholic news provider on the Asian continent.
- **AsiaNews:** As we saw above, AsiaNews is sponsored by the Pontifical Institute for Foreign Missions, a society of priests and laity founded in the mid-nineteenth century to support missionary activities abroad. It was launched in 2003, and its coverage of Asia in particular is extensive.
- **ACI Africa:** A news agency covering Church affairs across Africa, ACI Africa is an affiliate of ACI Prensa in Spanish and owned by EWTN. It was founded in 2019 and is headquartered in Nairobi, Kenya. ACI Africa has the same broad editorial policy as its parent platforms.

- **Radio Maria Africa:** According to UNESCO, radio stations are Africa's most popular information outlet, reaching far larger audiences than either traditional print publications or digital media platforms. Radio Maria Africa is the continent's largest Catholic radio network; it covers twenty-three stations in Africa, including outlets in the Democratic Republic of Congo, Rwanda, Burundi, and many other nations.

- **Radio Pacis:** Founded by a Comboni missionary in 2001 in the diocese of Aura in Uganda, located in the country's northwest and bordering South Sudan and Congo, Radio Pacis was named as a reference to the Ugandan Church's efforts at conflict resolution in Africa's Great Lakes region in the early 1990s. It's gone on to win awards from the BBC as the best radio station in Africa—not just Catholic, but overall—and is among the most influential Catholic media providers on the continent.

In terms of general observations, it's striking that all of these outlets are relatively new, with the oldest reaching back just to 1979. It's also worthy of note that four of the five are either actually edited outside Africa and Asia, or at least sponsored and controlled editorially by organizations based in either Europe or North America. What those two points suggest is that there's a great deal of undeveloped territory for independent and indigenous Catholic media in both Asia and Africa.

CHAPTER THREE

Case Study: The "Caso Boffo"

I've been covering the Vatican for the American market almost twenty-five years by this point, and that experience has brought home several hard truths. One is that there are certain stories that are fascinating, consequential, and full of unexpected twists and colorful characters, but that are simply way too Italian to ever successfully explain to an American audience. On my personal list of such stories over the years, a special pride of place goes to the 2009 drama of Dino Boffo, at the time the editor of *Avvenire*, the official newspaper of the Italian bishops' conference. In retrospect, the episode marked a turning point in the emergence of what we would today call the media's culture of contempt, in which political and theological differences fueled a vicious form of character assassination. So grotesque was the smear job that Italians even coined a new verb in its wake, "to Boffo someone," meaning to invent false and defamatory information against someone and spread it around so thick that the target eventually is fatally tainted, regardless of the truth of the situation.

To this day, *il Caso Boffo*, the "Boffo Case," is considered a leading example of what Italians call a *giallo*, an unresolved mystery.

As we've already discussed, what happens in Italy matters for the Catholic Church. Even if the vast majority of Catholics elsewhere have no idea who Dino Boffo is or what happened to him, the inner elite in the Church, including its journalistic elite, certainly does. In the end, the affair left everyone damaged, including senior figures in the Vatican; it also damaged the overall reputation of the Catholic Church. It created a template for the weaponization of political and theological differences, effectively marking the beginning of a new era regarding what Catholic media platforms are willing to put into public circulation.

It's important to draw the lessons from the Boffo affair, not only because it was among the first clear instances of the culture of contempt, but also because, for Americans, it provides us with a bit of critical distance in which it's not so much the personalities involved but the media dynamics that can be the focus of reflection.

WHAT HAPPENED

Born in northern Italy in 1952, Dino Boffo early on became involved in Catholic Action, by far the largest lay Catholic movement in the country. He became a protégé of the legendary Italian jurist and politician Vittorio Bachelet, a Christian Democrat who also led

Catholic Action until his assassination by Italy's leftist Red Brigades terrorist group in February 1980. Boffo went on to hold several leadership positions, earning a reputation as more culturally and politically conservative than the socially progressive form of Christian Democracy that Bachelet had represented. Among other things, he supported collaboration with Comunione e Liberazione (Communion and Liberation), a new movement founded by Fr. Luigi Giussani in 1954 and often seen as a right-wing rival to Catholic Action. At the time, Boffo also formed a friendship with a young Italian cleric named Camillo Ruini, who would later go on to become the Vicar of Rome under Pope John Paul II and president of the Italian bishops' conference.

In the 1980s Boffo began working as a journalist, becoming the deputy director of *Avvenire* in 1991 and director in 1994 after his predecessor died in a tragic car crash. Under his leadership, *Avvenire* was seen as tightly aligned with Ruini's culturally conservative vision—for example, backing Ruini's call in 2005 for Italians to abstain from a national referendum on legalizing IVF procedures. Boffo also fired a columnist who had suggested that under certain conditions, euthanasia ought to be permitted. On his watch, readership also went up, numerous inserts were launched, and a typographical overhaul of the print edition played to widely positive reviews. By all objective measures, by 2009 Boffo was at the top of his game, well wired in the leadership circles of the Italian Church and a seasoned media executive presiding over a good run for his flagship platform.

None of that success, however, insulated Boffo from the storm that broke open in late August 2009.

Shortly beforehand, *Avvenire* had published a series of commentary pieces critical of Italy's then–Prime Minister Silvio Berlusconi, not over policy but over Berlusconi's private conduct. At the time, Berlusconi was under fire amid what came to be known as the "Bunga Bunga" scandal, involving charges that young women were paid to attend parties at Berlusconi's Sardinian villa, while a high-class prostitute, who turned out to be underage, said she spent a night with him at his Rome residence. Basically, *Avvenire* suggested that such behavior set a poor moral tone for a public official, especially one who claims to promote Catholic values in his policies. It wasn't blistering stuff, but it did raise some eyebrows among Italians accustomed to thinking of Ruini and Berlusconi as strong allies.

The blowback was swift in coming. The conservative Italian daily *Il Giornale*, once owned by Berlusconi and, at the time, owned by his brother, published an alleged certificate of legal judgment from the Italian city of Terni in 2001–2002 that purported to show not only that Boffo was gay, but that he'd been fined for harassing phone calls to a woman because he wanted to carry on an affair with her husband. A set of purported judicial notes concluded that Boffo is "a known homosexual who has already come to the attention of the police for this kind of activity." Journalist Gabriele Villa, writing in *Il Giornale*, asserted, "The director of *Avvenire*, who's in the front row of the press campaign against Berlusconi, intimidated the wife of a man with whom he wanted to have a homosexual relationship. He bargained his way out of it: By paying a fine, he avoided six months in jail." The piece ran under the headline "The Super-Moralist Condemned for Molestations." (In reality, there never was any charge of physical molestation.)

In an accompanying editorial, the director of *Il Giornale* at the time, well-known Italian journalist Vittorio Feltri, wrote the following:

> The director of *Avvenire* does not have the credentials to launch furious anathemas at other sinners, real or presumed, nor even to pull Berlusconi's ears. The problem is that in the sexual arena, everyone has their weaknesses, and it's usually a good idea to avoid investigating those of someone else. Otherwise, you discover that the head of the moralists running around vituperating against the head of government is revealed to be like that ox who called the donkey a cuckold. Never like right now have we seen so many moralists, many of whom, if not almost all, don't have the suitable qualifications. The moment has arrived to unmask them.

Boffo immediately described the document as a fraud, and authorities in Terni confirmed that no such document existed. Instead, they said, Boffo had paid a fine of roughly $800 in 2004 after a complaint for harassing calls, but the finding had nothing to do with Boffo's alleged homosexuality. Boffo later claimed that he paid the fine to close a "painful incident" for a friend, and that he actually didn't make the calls in question. Nevertheless, the drumbeat of controversy led Boffo to resign his position at *Avvenire* as well as the official TV network of the Italian bishops, at the time known as Sat2000, and also their radio station, Radio inBlu.

Once it became clear that the purported court document was a fake, the question became who had put it into circulation and why. (The document had also been mailed anonymously to all the Italian bishops, suggesting not only that Boffo was guilty but that Ruini, along with Cardinal Diogini Tettamanzi of Milan and Archbishop Giuseppe Betori of Florence, "without doubt were aware of the offense.") Feltri himself said he obtained it from sources within the Vatican's security operation, and, while a Vatican spokesman dutifully denied the claim, it was nonetheless taken seriously by a broad swath of Italian opinion. Eventually, the leading theory became that the attack on Boffo originated with Pope Benedict XVI's Secretary of State, Italian Cardinal Tarcisio Bertone, who was upset with the criticism of Berlusconi in *Avvenire*, and who saw Ruini and his allies as rivals for control of the Italian Church. According to the theory, Bertone enlisted the head of the Vatican gendarmes, at the time Italian layman Domenico Giani, to come up with dirt on Boffo, and the editor of the Vatican newspaper, who was then Italian journalist and academic Giovanni Maria Vian, to spread it around quietly among his journalistic contacts. As such speculation made the rounds, the Vatican remained silent for eighteen long days, until it finally issued a formal denial. A leading Italian paper captured public reaction to the statement with the headline "Il Vaticano Nega Tutto, Nessuno Ci Crede," meaning "The Vatican Denies Everything, No One Believes It."

Three years later, we learned that Boffo, too, believed this theory. Amid the revelations of the first Vatileaks scandal in 2012 were two lengthy letters written by Boffo to then-Monsignor Georg Gänswein, the priest-secretary of Pope Benedict XVI, in which Boffo directly accused Bertone and Vian of being behind the plot to ruin him. Boffo asserted that Bertone resented his support for "continuity" in the Italian bishops' conference between its former president, the ultra-powerful Ruini, and his successor, Cardinal Angelo Bagnasco of Genoa. (At the time, Bertone aspired to replace the Italian bishops as the primary interlocutor with the Italian government.)

"I don't believe, to be honest with you, that Cardinal Bertone was informed of the details of the action conducted by Vian," Boffo told Gänswein, "but [Vian] perhaps could count, as in other situations, on accurately interpreting the mind of his superior."

Gänswein called Boffo after receiving the letter, after which Boffo wrote him again, this time largely to insist that he's not a homosexual. There was also a letter Boffo wrote to Bagnasco in September 2010, this time requesting rehabilitation. Boffo explicitly repeated his charges against Bertone and Vian. The letter also contained what can't help but seem a veiled threat. Noting that he had received numerous requests to give interviews, Boffo wrote he had declined because "if I speak, it's not as if I can skip over the part played by Bertone-Vian."

In all reality, however, this popular reconstruction never really passed the smell test. For one thing, whatever one may wish to believe about Bertone, who went on to be linked to a major financial scandal in the Vatican involving using funds supposedly donated for a children's hospital to remodel his private apartment, he certainly had easier means at his disposal had he wished to strike at Boffo. In all probability, a single phone call from the Secretariat of State would have seen Boffo sent packing. A similar point could be made about Giani, former chief of the Vatican gendarmes. Even if some might regard him as capable of participating in a smear job, it's unlikely he'd have been reckless enough to premise it on a document that could easily be demonstrated to be fake. Giani was a veteran of the Italian secret service, and undoubtedly he could have found more reliable means if he wanted someone out of the way.

Among other things, the Boffo episode highlighted a perceived crisis of governance in the Vatican under

Bertone, who effectively called the management shots under Pope Benedict XVI. It dumbfounded many observers that the Vatican could allow the narrative about the Boffo case to spin so badly out of control, converting what would have been perceived as a silly conspiracy theory in the public mind into something akin to Gospel truth. It was one of many examples during the Benedict papacy of scandals and train wrecks obscuring the pope's own message and activity, the cumulative effect of which almost certainly played a role in Benedict's decision to resign in February 2013. The affair triggered a drumbeat among many cardinals that the next pope would have to clean up the administrative mess, which would help sweep the Cardinal-Archbishop of Buenos Aires, Jorge Mario Bergoglio, into office.

To this day, it remains unknown who manufactured the fake legal judgment that triggered the scandal. Conventional wisdom, however, holds that it had to be someone close to Berlusconi, or at least someone supportive of Berlusconi even if he or she acted without his explicit consent. In other words, it seems a classic case of war—in this case, a war waged in the media, with misinformation being the main weapon—as a continuation, to cite Clausewitz, of politics by other means.

FALLOUT

For Boffo himself, now seventy, the consequences of the scandal continued to dog him for the rest of his career. Although he was named the director of TV2000, the Italian bishops' television network, in October 2010, he was then fired abruptly in 2014 with no official explanation ever given. By all accounts, the issues involved amounted to professional and managerial differences that had nothing directly to do with the scandal of 2009, but no doubt the perception that Boffo was weakened by the affair lurked in the background of why his superiors at the bishops' conference felt they could take such a preemptory step. As it turns out, Boffo had a nonfiring clause in his contract, one that no one at the conference had even invoked before, but after he filed a lawsuit, the conference was compelled to take him back as a home-based employee, which meant he was able to draw his full salary until he reached retirement age, which in Italy is typically sixty-seven. As a voice in Italian Catholic affairs, Boffo never returned to the reach and influence he'd enjoyed prior to the scandal.

For Feltri, the editor in chief of *Il Giornale*, which launched the scandal, he has always denied knowingly publishing a false document. Without revealing from whom it was obtained, Feltri has insisted that it was a credible Vatican source and he had no reason to doubt it was legitimate. Still, the affair seemed an obvious case of journalistic malpractice, since a few phone calls by a reporter to police and judicial officials in Terni almost certainly would have flagged the document as a fake prior to publication. The fact those phone calls weren't made in advance suggested to most observers that *Il Giornale* was more interested in discrediting Boffo than in establishing the facts. In 2010, Feltri was suspended from Italy's official register of journalists for six months, a punishment that was later reduced to three. However, it hardly marked the end of Feltri's relevance; he continued to be a prominent public figure in Italian affairs, and in 2015, he was even a serious candidate to become President of the Republic, finishing third in the round of balloting that elected Italy's current president, Sergio Mattarella. In 2021, he was elected to the city council in Milan.

As for the broader cultural significance of it, the affair gave birth to an expression still very much in use in Italian politics: the *Metodo Boffo*, or "Boffo Method," generally defined as a campaign of character assassination waged in the media, mixing truths with lies and manufactured misinformation, with the aim of not only discrediting a political adversary but also distracting public opinion from other issues that threaten whoever launched the campaign in the first place. Informally, the Boffo Method is also known in Italy as a *macchina di fango*, or "machine for throwing mud." In 2010, Marco Tarquinio, who succeeded Boffo at *Avvenire*, defined the Boffo Method as a sort of journalistic crime, a "conscious and violent way of doing harm."

Certainly, the legacy of the Boffo affair lives on in the minds of senior Church leaders from around the world who watched it play out. In 2019, Cardinal Óscar Rodriguez Maradiaga of Honduras, a member of the pope's council of cardinal advisors and one of his closest allies, invoked the phrase "Boffo Method" in an interview with the Italian press about new reports of Vatican financial scandals: "To me, it seems that what's going on more than anything else is a precise Boffo strategy to discredit us," Maradiaga said. "They want to strike the papacy. First, they depicted a church largely made up of pedophiles, now they're suggesting economic recklessness, but it's not so."

CATHOLIC IMPLICATIONS

One notable element of the Boffo affair is that it was driven almost entirely by politics rather than ideology, in that it wasn't a case of a camp representing one set of values and policy priorities attacking another. In broad strokes, the Italian bishops' conference under Ruini was in alignment with the Berlusconi government and its culturally conservative agenda, and certainly no one ever accused Boffo of being what Italians derisively call *un cattocomunista*, meaning "a Catholic communist." Instead, this was mostly a scorched-earth battle within an ideological camp, with the issue being how absolute one's loyalty should be to a leader on the basis of his policy positions and to the exclusion of any consideration of his or her personal moral standing or fitness for office. That question continues to resonate to this day, with contrasting conservative Catholic attitudes toward former President Donald Trump serving as a very current case in point.

This isn't a story about the Catholic press in the direct sense, given that it was a secular outlet that launched the anti-Boffo campaign. In Italy, however, the distinction between "Catholic" and "secular" is notoriously fuzzy, and clearly it was the Catholic press here and abroad that took the greatest interest. For the Catholic press, the Boffo case served as an early warning system for tectonic shifts that would gather force over the years to come. It revealed a sinister logic that has only become steadily more evident in what Catholic media outlets are willing to publish, and how careless they may be in ensuring information is legitimate before broadcasting it. The logic rests on two premises: (1) Positions considered erroneous on either ecclesiastical or political issues generally reveal some personal skeleton in the closet (e.g., someone who supports greater outreach to homosexuals in the Church is probably gay themselves). (2) It's not only legitimate to publicize those skeletons in the closet but also a matter of duty to do so as a means of combatting the errors the person in question upholds.

To be clear, there's nothing wrong with investigative journalism that reveals the hypocrisy or misconduct of public officials. Yet, in theory, journalists ought to have a high bar regarding the publication of damaging information about individual persons. Among the standards should be that the individual in question is a public figure who has voluntarily renounced a degree of the privacy rights that ordinary people should enjoy; that the information is clearly in the public interest; and that every effort has been made to ensure not only that the information is accurate but that the individual has had opportunities to present his or her side of the story before publication or broadcast.

None of those standards seemed met in the Boffo case. Granted, Boffo was the editor of the Italian bishops' newspaper, and someone who frequently editorialized on public matters. Yet it's a bit of a journalistic conceit to conclude that this automatically makes him a "public figure," since I'd be willing to guess that prior to this episode, most Italians had never heard of Boffo and couldn't pick him out in a lineup. In reality, Boffo occupied a stratum we might call "semi-public figures," and certainly had a greater expectation of privacy than, say, a bishop or a Vatican official. That is to say, just because he was a big deal in journalistic circles doesn't mean he was a "public figure" in the classic sense. In other words, the target of such a damaging report should already be a public figure—it shouldn't be the report that makes them one.

Beyond that, it's also obvious there was a reckless disregard for the truth in the Boffo case. As we have seen, no one bothered to verify the accuracy of the alleged court document before publication, nor did anyone reach out to Boffo to ask for an explanation. Presumably, excitement over the supposed bombshell revelation, coupled with a sense of its importance in the effort to defend Berlusconi against his critics, overwhelmed the usual firebreaks to publication. That's a pattern hardly confined to the Catholic press, of course, but Boffo was the first time it was directed against a specifically Catholic target.

In sum, the Boffo case marked a turning point in the emergence of contempt as a driving force in journalistic decision-making. While Boffo himself may have been semi-vindicated, the media template that now bears his name was the big winner in the affair, because it set new standards that have only been solidified as time has gone on.

CHAPTER FOUR

Case Study: The Ratzinger Narrative

In both specialized media studies and common par-
lance, the term "narrative" is widely used today to
describe the cluster of impressions, assumptions, and
a priori biases that surround a particular figure or issue
in media coverage and public conversation. In general,
the "narrative" is understood to be highly influential in
how the media approaches a particular story, shaping
the way new developments or facts are understood.
Though one can find plenty of specialized academic
definitions of "narrative," perhaps the best expression
of it I've ever seen comes from novelist Stephen Hunter,
who writes the popular Bob Lee Swagger series of novels
about a former sniper turned righter-of-wrongs. At one
point in the 2009 novel *I, Sniper*, Swagger finds himself
attempting to exonerate a former Marine sniper accused
of having killed four people, and he enlists the help of a
friend who warns him of the magnitude of the challenge
they face.

"Let me tell you what's going on, and why this one is so touchy," the friend says. "We are fighting the narrative. You do not fight the narrative. The narrative will destroy you. The narrative is all-powerful. The narrative rules. It rules us, it rules Washington, it rules everything. Now ask me, 'What is the narrative?'"

"What is the narrative?" Swagger asks.

"The narrative is the set of assumptions the press believes in, possibly without even knowing that it believes in them," the friend says. "It's so powerful because it's unconscious. It's not like they get together every morning and decide, 'These are the lies we tell today.' No, that would be too crude and honest. Rather, it's a set of casual, non-rigorous assumptions about a reality they've never really experienced that's arranged in such a way as to reinforce their best and most ideal presumptions about themselves and their importance to the system and the way they've chosen to live their lives. It's a way of arranging things a certain way that they all believe in without ever really addressing carefully. . . .

"The narrative is the bedrock of their culture, the keystone of their faith, the altar of their church. They don't even know they're true believers, because in theory they despise the true believer in anything. But they will absolutely de-frackin'-stroy anybody who makes them question all that, and Nick had the temerity to do so, even if he didn't quite realize it at the time. I don't know who or what's behind it, but I do know this: they have all the cards, and if you play in that game, they will destroy you too."

"Why can't we simply destroy the narrative?" Swagger asks.

"Starling, it's everywhere. It's all things. It's permanent. It's beyond. It's beneath. It's above. It's in the air, the music, the furniture, the DNA, the blood, if these [blank]s had blood."

"I say, 'Destroy the narrative,'" Swagger insists.

"I say, 'You will yourself be destroyed.'"

This is a novel we're talking about, so the description of the narrative is obviously a bit overdrawn. Most reporters I've known over the years are actually capable of being critical of their own assumptions at least once in a while. Still, there's a great deal of truth to the idea that media representations of a situation often reflect *a priori* narratives as much as they do factual reality. Moreover, the allure of the narrative isn't always unconscious; sometimes reporters know full well that if they supply a story that feeds the narrative, it'll draw bigger and more immediate audiences than one that doesn't.

One classic example of how narratives can distort reality, even fueling contempt for people who challenge the narrative, is in coverage of Pope Benedict XVI, the former Cardinal Joseph Ratzinger. Though I have no empirical evidence to support this claim, no peer-reviewed longitudinal media studies to back it up, I'll nevertheless say that in my experience, no public official in the twenty-first century has ever entered office surrounded by a worse public narrative than Pope Benedict. For sure, no leader in our time, and possibly ever, endured a more dramatic disjunction between their public persona and their private personality.

THE RATZINGER NARRATIVE

I came on the Catholic beat in the early 1990s, at a time when Ratzinger was at the peak of his powers as Pope John Paul II's doctrinal czar. As Prefect of the Congregation for the Doctrine of the Faith, there was no public controversy in the Catholic Church over a quarter-century in which Ratzinger was not a protagonist, from battles over liberation theology in Latin America in the 1970s and '80s to gay rights and women's issues in the 1990s. It was Ratzinger, for example, who issued the memorable decree in 1986 describing homosexuality as a "tendency ordered toward an intrinsic moral evil" and the homosexual inclination itself as an "objective disorder," language that, to this day, is cited by critics as virtually a form of hate speech. It was also Ratzinger who drew lines in the sand over the limits of theological dissent, and who insisted that bishops' conferences, the signature post–Vatican II exercise in collegiality, have no teaching authority on their own.

In Catholic circles, it's almost impossible to over-state how large Ratzinger loomed. For some, he was the heroic defender of the faith, the figure with the courage to draw lines in the sand and to call heresy and error by their true names. For others, he became the symbol of all they disliked about the Church, a benighted prelate using the power of the papacy to enforce an archconservative agenda on Catholicism completely at odds with the Second Vatican Council. In those circles, one could almost hear the Imperial Death March from Star Wars playing in people's minds whenever Ratzinger's name was even mentioned. In the public mind, this was *Herr Panzerkardinal*, "God's Rottweiler," the "German Shepherd," and any number of other derogatory epithets that had grown up over the years.

Those prejudices surrounding Ratzinger were memorably captured by an editorial cartoon in one of Italy's leading leftist newspapers the day after his election as Pope Benedict XVI in April 2005. The cartoon was a play on one of the most iconic moments from the papacy of St. John XXIII, *il Papa buono*, or "the good pope," as Italians still call him to this day. On October 11, 1962, John XXIII came to the window of the papal apartments looking out over St. Peter's Square to address a crowd that gathered carrying torches and candles to celebrate the opening of the Second Vatican Council. Gazing out over the thousand points of light, Pope John launched into an impromptu reflection in which he said that the whole world was represented in the square that night, and that even the moon seemed to have stopped in its tracks to look down on the scene.

Then, at the end, he delivered the line that's still burned into the collective Italian memory, that's taught in schools and referenced in a thousand and one ways in popular culture. It went like this: "When you get home tonight, you'll find your children. Give them a kiss and tell them, 'This is the kiss of the pope.'"

So, the editorial cartoon the day after Benedict XVI's election displayed the new pope once again standing at the window overlooking St. Peter's Square on a moonlit night; only this time, the message was slightly different: "When you go home tonight, you'll find your children. Give them a spanking and tell them that this spanking is from the pope!"

Such was the narrative surrounding Joseph Ratzinger at the time. Let's face it: from the point of view of much of the press, Ratzinger was straight out of central casting as a villain: he speaks English with a German accent that reminds Americans of every Nazi bad guy they've ever seen in the movies, he's perceived as doctrinaire and aloof, and he's a cultural conservative in a regal cassock with a shock of snow-white hair and a pair of pince-nez glasses slid halfway down, which always made it seem as if he was sort of looking down his nose at people. He also, of course, happened to symbolize what one side of the Church's ideological debates, and their secular allies, saw as ruin. Honestly, it would have been a miracle had his narrative not been toxic.

Substantively, the indictment generally rests on four core premises. First, that Ratzinger either was a Nazi at some point, or was at least sympathetic to the Nazis. So steeped was this idea in the popular consciousness that the actress Susan Sarandon, who starred in the 1995 anti–capital punishment movie *Dead Man Walking*, once casually called Benedict XVI a Nazi in a public address, taking it to be established conventional wisdom. Sarandon was addressing a film festival in New York, and she told the audience that she'd sent a copy of the book upon which *Dead Man Walking* was based to the pope at the time. "The last one," Sarandon said. "Not this Nazi we have now." The line came in an interview conducted by fellow actor Bob Balaban about Sarandon's career that was part of the Hamptons Film Festival. Although Balaban gently chided Sarandon, who was raised as a Catholic in New York, she actually repeated the remark.

Although both Jewish and Catholic groups objected, what's telling about the incident is that it was six years into Benedict's papacy, after his history in Nazi Germany had been thoroughly examined and debunked, and yet the impression of his Nazi affinities remained so strong it could be repeated publicly without justification or gloss.

Second, that Ratzinger is not only an archconservative but a revanchist seeking to reverse or overturn the Second Vatican Council. That accusation dates to 1985, when then-Cardinal Ratzinger gave a book-length interview to renowned Italian Catholic journalist Vittorio Messori, published in Italian as *Rapporto sulla Fede* and in English as *The Ratzinger Report*. It's again telling, by the way, that the English publishers apparently believed that putting Ratzinger's name in the title would help push it off shelves, which is one index of his celebrity status in the Catholic Church at the time.

Ten years before the book, Ratzinger had already described the decade following Vatican II as "a period of ecclesiastical decadence, in which the people who had started it later on became incapable of stopping the avalanche." In the book, however, he outlined his critique of the way implementation of the council had occurred in his typically crystalline and trenchant manner, generating perhaps the greatest fault line in the John Paul II era. So pronounced was the divide that when John Paul II called a Synod of Bishops in 1985 to ponder the council's twentieth anniversary, all the questions at the opening press conference were about *The Ratzinger Report*. A frustrated Vatican spokesman at one point lost his cool, exclaiming, "This is a synod about a council, not about a book!"

What especially rankles critics in this regard is the perception that Ratzinger was once a liberal, during the council itself, but later sold his soul in order to climb the career ladder in the Catholic Church. As one liberal German theologian and former Ratzinger colleague once put it, the future pope developed "scarlet fever," meaning a lust for the scarlet robes that mark the office of a cardinal.

Third, critics assert that Joseph Ratzinger symbolizes everything wrong with the Catholic Church's failures on child sexual abuse, from the inability to project genuine empathy for victims to unwillingness to undertake the needed reforms. In addition, some have also accused Ratzinger of engaging in abuse cover-ups himself when he was the Archbishop and, later, the Cardinal of Munich from 1977 to 1982. So chronic is that image that when survivors of sexual abuse by Catholic clergy and their advocates stage protests in front of church properties, some of the demonstrators inevitably will carry images of Pope Benedict with "wanted" under his picture, suggesting that he ought to be behind bars.

Finally, it's said that Ratzinger is cold, aloof, draconian, and harsh, a sort of Dostoyevskian Grand Inquisitor with the power of the Vatican to back him up. When he served as the Archbishop of Munich from 1977 to 1982, he was known for communicating with his priests through letters rather than personal encounters, fueling impressions of a figure distant from real people and consumed with theological abstractions. During his quarter-century in Rome, Ratzinger was known for avoiding interviews and most public appearances, preferring to pass his time in his office at the Congregation for the Doctrine of the Faith.

Spoofs of Ratzinger on Italian TV would often depict an isolated, reactionary potentate sitting alone in a marble-and-gold palace, detached from the reality unfolding in the streets all around him. A standard gag depicted an aide trying to explain some completely commonsense thing to him—for instance, that Italians were striking over stagnant wages amid their latest cycle of inflation and economic crisis—while the white-haired autocrat professes total incomprehension.

When the *New York Times* profiled the new Pope Benedict XVI in 2005, here's what one young German, thirty-five-year-old Christian Schuster, had to say: "He'll never be able to connect with young people like John Paul. The pope had humility. Cardinal Ratzinger has a different image. He is a very powerful man."

While these images became fixed in the popular mind due to their diffusion in the secular media, they started in the Catholic press. It was Catholic journalists who described Ratzinger in these terms in their essays and reports, and who recycled these prejudices in both their interviews and private conversations with their secular colleagues. Indeed, one can say that it was the presumed expertise and insight of specialized Catholic journalists, and Catholic commentators quoted by secular journalists, who made the Ratzinger narrative possible and who sustained it long after the weight of evidence should have brought it crashing down. In that sense, the Ratzinger narrative is a classic example of the culture of contempt at work, in which political and theological disagreements become a pretext for character assassination and personal smears.

REALITY V. IMAGE

Ratzinger and the Nazis

We don't have to dwell on this charge very long, because it's got to be already one of the most thoroughly debunked canards in recent history. To state the facts briefly, Joseph Ratzinger was six years old when Adolph Hitler became the Chancellor of Germany in 1933, and he was therefore eighteen when the Thousand Year Reich fell. At no point was the young Ratzinger or anyone in his family a member of the Nazi Party. Indeed, his father, also named Joseph, was a minor police official in Bavaria who voluntarily accepted a series of less significant appointments in various small Bavarian towns in order not to have to collaborate with the Brown Shirts, and he eventually went into early retirement. Ratzinger and his brother, Georg, continued their seminary studies as long as possible until, in 1943, Ratzinger, along with his entire seminary class, was drafted into the anti-aircraft corps. When that service concluded, Ratzinger was drafted into the regular army, the *Wehrmacht*, and assigned to a base near the border with Hungary where his unit laid out tank traps. In 1945, Ratzinger deserted, and he experienced a brief stint as an American prisoner of war before being released.

At no point during this time did Ratzinger ever demonstrate any enthusiasm for the Nazi cause. In 1941, membership in the Hitler Youth became mandatory for all German youth, and Ratzinger was forcibly enrolled.

But he never even picked up his membership card, and a sympathetic teacher allowed him to continue attending school without it. In all honesty, there was never much likelihood the Ratzinger family would have been drawn to National Socialism, even before its horrors became common knowledge. For one thing, they lived in the orbit of Salzburg and its French-influenced Catholic culture, not the stern abstemiousness of the Prussian north in Germany. The Ratzingers were proud of this legacy; prior to Benedict XVI, the most famous member of the family was Georg Ratzinger, the future pontiff's great-uncle, who served two terms in the Bavarian regional legislature. For another, the Ratzingers are by temperament exceedingly gentle, reserved personalities, and the thuggishness and bombast of the Brown Shirts would have been deeply appalling to them.

Bottom line: Joseph Ratzinger was never a Nazi. Even if one insists on his brief and compulsory enrollment in the Hitler Youth, that's not the same thing as membership in the Nazi party. One can certainly argue that a person of conscience in Nazi Germany should have done more to make his or her dissent clear, and there were examples of such active resistance in the immediate vicinity of the Ratzingers, including the famous White Rose circle at the University of Munich. The fact that someone chose to dissent largely by focusing on preparations for the priesthood rather than political protest, however, in no way makes them a collaborator with the regime.

Ratzinger and the Second Vatican Council

No element of the "black legend" surrounding Joseph Ratzinger is more enduring than that he betrayed the legacy of the Second Vatican Council, that reforming summit of more than two thousand Catholic bishops from around the world that launched the Catholic Church on a program of modernization. Ratzinger participated in the council as a *peritus*, or theological expert, for Cardinal Josef Frings of Cologne, where he was seen as part of the broad progressive majority seeking change. Later he moved in a more conservative direction, with many of his colleagues and peers suggesting he did so to acquire ecclesiastical power and status. With every step up the career ladder, that drumbeat of criticism became steadily louder, to the point that it took on the status of something approaching conventional wisdom.

In all reality, however, it's not that Ratzinger changed spots, starting out as a liberal and then opportunistically shifting to the right as the winds in the Catholic Church began to blow in a different direction. Instead, it's that the Ratzinger of the council had a different vision of the council's purpose and achievement, and he would remain loyal to that vision throughout his career and into his papacy.

Because the progressives were the strong majority at Vatican II, their galaxy contained multiple planets. One of the most important distinctions ran between the camps of *aggiornamento* (updating) and *ressourcement* (back to the sources). Both were in enthusiastic agreement that the fossilized form the Catholic Church had taken on by the late 1950s needed to be replaced, but they differed in where they drew their inspiration for that reform. Advocates of aggiornamento looked forward to the modern world, seeking to reconcile the Catholic Church with secularity, while the upholders of ressourcement looked back to the original sources of the faith, especially the early Church Fathers.

Maybe a comparison will help. Suppose you're a baseball fan watching a game between the Dodgers and the Giants, or the Cardinals and the Cubs, or, of course, the Yankees and the Red Sox. Those are probably baseball's most storied rivalries, with fan bases that genuinely dislike one another, and the games between those teams always tend to be intense. But no matter which team you're cheering for, you'd see this as a contest within baseball. I mean, it's not as if the Dodgers are going to suddenly break out hockey sticks, or the Cubs are going to run down fly balls on polo horses. Both teams are fully committed to the game; the only difference is that they want their side to win and the other to lose.

Ratzinger was always destined to be seen as a "conservative" in post–Vatican II, secular terms, because the ressourcement instinct was never interested in sweeping doctrinal changes. The issues that came to dominate in liberal Western Catholic circles after the council, such as Church teaching on birth control, abortion, and homosexuality, were never on their radar screens. They took the ancient formulas of the faith as givens and were primarily interested in reviving elements of early Christian faith and practice that they felt had been neglected over the centuries. Many of these figures later coalesced into what would be known as the "Communio" school, after the name of the theological journal they founded, which stood in contrast to "Concilium," the journal launched by the more aggiornamento-oriented thinkers at the council.

In other words, Ratzinger was never an opponent of Vatican II, and he rejected the genuinely traditionalist camp in the Church that refused to embrace the council's teachings, not just on liturgy but on ecumenism, interfaith dialogue, the separation of church and state, and a whole host of other matters. Instead, Ratzinger took one side in a contest after the council ended, involving people who were all supporters of the council, and many of whom had been protagonists during its session, to define the council's legacy and real import. Put differently, Ratzinger never challenged Vatican II, and indeed his papacy would eventually be largely inspired by its decisions. What he challenged was what he considered an incorrect interpretation of Vatican II, one that, to put it colloquially, threatened to throw out the baby with the bathwater, emptying Christianity of its doctrinal content in favor of an ever-shifting détente with the zeitgeist. Far from betraying Vatican II, Ratzinger would probably say he's been trying to save it from others who, consciously or not, are betraying it themselves.

Portraying Ratzinger as an enemy of the council, therefore, always has been a contemptuous way of describing his position. He's an enemy of more progressive readings of the council, but that's a fight within the family of the children of Vatican II.

Ratzinger and Sex Abuse

There's no doubt that far later than he probably should have been, Ratzinger remained in denial about the scope and scale of the sexual abuse crisis in the Catholic Church. For more than two decades after his arrival in Rome in 1981, there's no evidence that Ratzinger as the Prefect of the Congregation for the Doctrine of the Faith and a key advisor to Pope John Paul II broke with the standard Vatican attitude at the time—that while priests may occasionally do reprehensible things, talk of a "crisis" was the product of a media and legal campaign to wound the Church. Ratzinger's attitude toward the crisis at the time can perhaps best be gauged from comments he made on November 30, 2002, during an appearance in Murcia, Spain, at a conference organized by the Catholic University of St. Anthony. During a Q&A session after his talk, Ratzinger was asked: "This past year has been difficult for Catholics, given the space dedicated by the media to scandals attributed to priests. There is talk of a campaign against the church. What do you think?"

This was Ratzinger's reply:

> In the church, priests are also sinners. But I am personally convinced that the constant presence in the press of the sins of Catholic priests, especially in the United States, is a planned campaign, as the percentage of these offenses among priests is not higher than in other categories, and perhaps it is even lower. In the United States, there is constant news on this topic, but less than one percent of priests are guilty of acts of this type. The constant presence of these news items does not correspond to the objectivity of the information or to the statistical objectivity of the facts. Therefore, one comes to the conclusion that it is intentional, manipulated, that there is a desire to discredit the church.

Note that the "less than one percent" claim was based on research carried out in just one American diocese, the Archdiocese of Chicago, which covered only the period up to 1991, and which examined only case files without seeking unreported incidents. Making Ratzinger's defensive tone all the more striking, his comments came after a summit between Vatican officials and American cardinals, as well as officers of the bishops' conference, in April 2002 to discuss the American crisis, a meeting in which Ratzinger participated.

Yet that late 2002 rhetoric was, in a sense, already an echo of the past rather than a portent of the future.

Around that time, Ratzinger's attitude began to shift decisively, and before long he would emerge as the Eliot Ness of the Catholic Church on the sex abuse front, the lone senior Vatican official for the better part of a decade who took the problem seriously and who pushed aggressively for tougher measures to combat it. By all accounts, the turning point in Ratzinger's attitude came in May 2001, with a legal document from John Paul II titled *Sacramentorum Sanctitatis Tutela*. Technically known as a *motu proprio*, the document assigned juridical responsibility for certain grave crimes under canon law, including sexual abuse of a minor, to Ratzinger's congregation. It also compelled diocesan bishops all over the world to forward their case files to Rome, where the congregation would make a decision about the appropriate course of action.

Maltese Bishop Charles Scicluna, who served under Ratzinger as the Promoter of Justice in the Congregation for the Doctrine of the Faith—in effect, its lead prosecutor—and who's now the Bishop of Malta, said in an interview with *Avvenire* that the *motu proprio* triggered an "avalanche" of files in Rome, most of which arrived in 2003 and 2004. Eventually, Scicluna said, more than three thousand cases worked their way through the congregation.

Ratzinger was punctilious about studying the files, making him one of the few churchmen anywhere in the world to have read the documentation on virtually every Catholic priest ever credibly accused of sexual abuse. As a result, he acquired a familiarity with the contours of the problem that virtually no other figure in the Catholic Church can claim. Driven by that encounter with what he would later refer to as "filth" in the Church, Ratzinger seems to have undergone something of a "conversion experience" throughout 2003–04. From that point forward, he and his staff seemed driven by a convert's zeal to clean up the mess.

Ratzinger's transformation can also be glimpsed from an exchange with Cardinal Francis George of Chicago, which George described in April 2005, just after the conclave that propelled Benedict XVI to the papacy. Two days before the opening of the conclave, George met Ratzinger in his Vatican office to discuss the American sex abuse norms, including the "one strike and you're out" policy. Those norms had been approved grudgingly in late 2002 by the Vatican, and only for a five-year period. George said he wanted to discuss with Ratzinger the arguments for making the norms permanent. Ratzinger, according to George, showed "a good grasp of the situation."

Forty-eight hours later, Ratzinger was the new pope. As is the custom, the cardinals gathered in the Sistine Chapel made their way, one by one, to the new pontiff in order to pledge their support and obedience. As George kissed his hand, Benedict XVI made a point of telling him, in English, that he remembered the conversation the two men had had about the sexual abuse norms and would attend to it. The new pope's first words to a senior

American prelate, in other words, were a vow of action on the clerical abuse crisis.

As pope, Benedict XVI moved swiftly to make good on his promise. Just one month after his election, the new pope removed Fr. Gino Burresi, a charismatic Italian priest and founder of the Servants of the Immaculate Heart of Mary, from his position and barred him from all public ministry. While the decree cited abuses of confession and spiritual direction, Vatican sources were clear that accusations of sexual abuse involving Burresi and seminarians, dating to the 1970s and '80s, were a principal motive for the action against him. A few months later, the same axe fell against a much bigger target: Mexican Fr. Marcial Maciel Degollado, founder of the controversial Legion of Christ.

Benedict would go on to codify the special American norms on abuse into the universal law of the Church, making "zero tolerance" more or less the global norm. He expelled hundreds of abusers from the priesthood, became the first pope to meet with survivors of clerical abuse (on a trip to the United States in 2008), and was the first pope to apologize in his own voice for the abuse crisis. In the Vatican itself, before Benedict took office, deniers of the abuse crisis were the tone-setting majority and the reformers a sort of courageous but embattled guerilla movement. By the time he was done, the deniers had been driven underground and the reformers had a full grip on the reins of power.

To be sure, there was unfinished business. Most prominently, Ratzinger always seemed to treat the abuse crisis as a problem of wayward priests, not always recognizing that the issue also involved negligent or corrupt bishops who looked the other way. Measures to hold leadership accountable for those failures were not adopted on Benedict's watch and, frankly, remain a work in progress under Pope Francis. Moreover, Benedict often failed to project the empathy for survivors that he undoubtedly felt, coming off as defensive even when he didn't mean to. He lacked, in a word, Francis' pastoral knack for reaching people emotionally as well as intellectually and in terms of policy.

All that said, there is no basis for suggesting that Pope Benedict XVI was, or remains, "part of the problem" when it comes to the fight against clerical sexual abuse. To the extent that charge ever had merit, it stopped being true almost twenty years ago—all of which, perhaps, suggests more about the power of a narrative to endure once it's set in stone than it does about the track record of an oft-misunderstood pope.

Ratzinger the Man

In all honesty, anyone who's ever met Pope Benedict XVI will testify that he's an unfailingly kind, gentle, and unassuming personality, making his reputation for arrogance all the more inexplicable. Here's one quick story out of a countless number of possibilities to make the point.

I first met then-Cardinal Joseph Ratzinger in 1999, while he was still at the height of his powers at the Congregation for the Doctrine of the Faith, and while I was a newly minted Catholic journalist working in the Kansas City newsroom of the *National Catholic Reporter*. I've always been a bit precocious, and so I decided to write a biography of Ratzinger even though I'd never met the man, I'd never covered a single story in the Vatican at that point, and I barely read German. Nevertheless, so many of the stories we covered back then pivoted on Ratzinger, and it occurred to me that there was no readily available biography in English. I dutifully put in an interview request with Ratzinger's Vatican office, though since I represented a newspaper known to be hostile to much of Ratzinger's agenda, I wasn't expecting much.

After a while, I got a phone call from someone at the Congregation for the Doctrine of the Faith informing me that an interview wouldn't be possible. However, this official let me know that His Eminence would be traveling shortly to San Francisco for a consultation among the heads of the doctrine committees of English-speaking bishops' conferences, and that he'd be giving a news conference at the end. If I was interested, the official said, I could go to San Francisco and at least take part in the media scrum. I swiftly made my plans, thinking that I could cover the doctrinal consultation while I was there, interview a few bishops, and get a story for *NCR* out of it as well. Though it wasn't clear to us at the time, our host, then-Archbishop William Levada, would eventually take over for Ratzinger at the CDF after his election to the papacy.

I arrived on the campus of St. Patrick's Seminary on day one of the meeting, and I quickly found the atmosphere far more cordial and relaxed than I had expected. (Part of the reason, looking back, is that Aussies and Kiwis were involved, who aren't ones generally to stand on ceremony.) At one point, Ratzinger was the main celebrant at a public Mass held in the seminary's chapel, and that night he was to be the guest of honor at a seminary reception. Naturally I showed up, expecting, I suppose, that when the great man entered the hall, trumpets would blast and everyone would fall to their knees in obeisance. Instead, at one point I happened to see two figures quietly slip in one of the doors, and it took me a couple of minutes to realize it was Ratzinger and his priest-secretary, who at the time was still Monsignor Josef Klemens. Ratzinger took off his coat and stood meekly until Levada realized he was there, and he was then whisked away to give greetings to seminarians and some elegantly dressed laity I could only imagine to be fat-cat seminary donors.

As time wore on, people started drifting away. Eventually, I was one of the few people left in the hall, at a time when Ratzinger, clearly worn out by the evening, dropped onto a sofa for a few moments' rest. Spotting me nearby, he waved me over to invite me to join him. Klemens was there too, and he explained to

Ratzinger that I was the American journalist working on a biography. He replied with a wry smile, joking that he could hardly believe his life was worth the effort of an entire book.

"I am sorry it was not possible to arrange an interview," he said, in his precise German-inflected English. "I have so many requests, and I must be disciplined. But we are here now, so if there is anything you would like to ask me informally, I have a few moments."

Flustered at the unexpected windfall, I wasn't quite sure where to begin, but I managed to croak out something like the following: "We're at a seminary, which reminds me that you were a professional college theologian for a long time, part of the club. Does it bother you that so many of your former friends and colleagues have become so critical of you?"

He smiled again, and then gave his answer. I can't remember it word for word because we were on background and I wasn't recording the conversation, but the gist was that in the seventeenth century, the Vatican had a problem with Jansenism, a theological movement that stressed original sin and human depravity and resulted in a pretty bleak view of human nature and freedom. Ratzinger said the Vatican had to intervene to correct the errors in Jansenism, and, he added, it's really not clear how many Jansenists changed their minds at the time because of what the Vatican said and did. Still, he said, three centuries later, Jansenism is no longer a living force in the Church.

Honestly, it took me a second to figure out whether Ratzinger had just answered my question or not. Eventually, it dawned on me that he had; his point was that sometimes Church authority is forced to take a stand, and doing so doesn't always produce immediate results, or at least not the ones you may have desired. Some irritation, even among people who were once your friends, is to be expected. Over time, however, things will sort themselves out, and it's important not to be overly invested in the here-and-now. (That bit of perspective, among other things, was a classic example of what people in and around the Vatican refer to as the fine art of "thinking in centuries.")

By the way, one can certainly challenge the point Ratzinger was making; sometimes, frankly, too much indifference to reaction in the here-and-now can signal a tone-deafness that's at odds with meeting people where they are. The point, however, is that Ratzinger was under no obligation to open himself up to me like that, and, frankly, many other Vatican potentates wouldn't have let a precocious American cub reporter get within one hundred feet of them without calling a Vatican gendarme. It was almost as if discourtesy was physically repugnant to Ratzinger, while being kind was second nature.

Another irony, by the way, is that the image of Ratzinger as a sort of draconian brute may have been the prejudice from the outside, but inside the Vatican it was always exactly the opposite: he was seen as too gentle, too kind, too soft, to govern effectively. In other words, *ad extra* critics said he was too harsh, while *ad intra* detractors said he wasn't nearly harsh enough, often betrayed by aides with whom he had an excess of patience and overly tolerant of corrupt or incompetent Vatican officials who should have been given the bum's rush a long time ago. He couldn't win for losing, excoriated in the media every time he tried to impose even modest discipline on someone, and lampooned behind his back in the corridors of power when he didn't crack heads.

Conclusion: Think what you will about the policies and theological convictions of Pope Benedict XVI, both of which are eminently open to debate—a point, by the way, he would be the first to concede. To suggest that he is some sort of Darth Vader in a cassock, however, is, well, contemptuous—making Benedict's public reputation just another casualty of the culture of contempt, in this case aided and abetted by a great deal of Catholic commentary.

CHAPTER FIVE

Case Study: The Bergoglio Counternarrative

What a difference a change at the top can make. In just a few weeks in the spring of 2013, the Catholic Church went from being shepherded by a pope with perhaps the ugliest public narrative of any world leader, to a new pontiff with the best narrative on the entire global stage. Not only did Pope Francis' "man of the people" profile electrify Catholics around the world, but even hard-core secularists couldn't help but be charmed. Within months, Francis was not only on the cover of the Italian edition of *Vanity Fair*, but he was *Time* magazine's "Person of the Year." (That's an honor bestowed upon only two previous popes, John XXIII and John Paul II, and both had to wait years into their papacies to get it.) He actually beat out George Clooney to be declared *Esquire*'s "Best Dressed Man" in 2013, where editors were beguiled by his simple attire, and, after his celebrated "Who am I to judge?" line about gay priests, he was even displayed on the cover of the pro-gay magazine *The Advocate*, showing the pope's smiling face with a "NOH8" sticker.

A July 2013 trip to Brazil cemented his celebrity status when Francis drew more than 3 million people for a Mass at Rio de Janeiro's Copacabana Beach, shattering the previous attendance record on the world's most famous stretch of sand and surf—a record held, by the way, by the Rolling Stones. It was another moment during his week-long stay in Brazil, however, that best captured the ferment around the man.

On Wednesday, July 24, Francis headed off to the Brazilian shrine of Our Lady of Aparecida, the most popular Marian sanctuary in Latin America. It's a site close to the heart of the pope, not only because of his strong devotion to the Blessed Virgin Mary but also because it was the setting for a summit of Latin American bishops in 2007 where then-Cardinal Jorge Mario Bergoglio of Argentina was the lead author of a document calling on Catholics to recover their missionary drive, a text that now serves as the Magna Carta of his papacy. It's so important to Francis that he's presented a copy of the Aparecida Document to every Latin American head of state he's met since his election.

Riding the pope-mobile as he arrived that day, Francis was delivered to the rear of the sanctuary in an area that supposedly had been cordoned off as a secure zone. Despite the rope lines and massive police presence, however, a group of roughly forty Brazilian nuns had somehow managed to worm their way into the space.

When the door to the pope-mobile popped open and Francis appeared, they lunged forward, shrieking and crying for all the world like teenage girls at a Justin Bieber concert. "Nuns gone wild!" was the instant headline around the world, with an amused Francis willingly standing in the courtyard exchanging hugs, wiping away tears of joy from the nuns' eyes, and posing for a seemingly endless round of selfies.

Within months, the media narrative about Pope Francis was set: he's a humble man of the people, a progressive reformer and a maverick, and a man of conviction and vision, and, to the extent there's opposition, it comes from a Vatican old guard allergic to change, conservative American bishops threatened by a loss of their power, and a disgruntled traditionalist wing of the Catholic Church that's simply unwilling to move with the times. So powerful did that narrative become that, by now, most media organizations have invested far too much time and treasure in recycling it to really entertain any serious challenge to it. I've seen this dynamic at work a thousand times: In the Benedict era, a negative story about the pope would get significant attention from the mainstream media (for instance, the abuse crisis) while positive stories (for example, Benedict's extensive teaching on the environment) often were buried. In the Francis era, the dynamic is exactly the opposite: positive stories, such as the pope cold-calling a young kid who'd written him a letter, blow up, while negative stories, such as the setbacks and failures in his financial reform of the Vatican, struggle to find traction.

As a result, Francis' broad popularity remains largely undimmed, defying expectations that his "honeymoon" would have to end. A June 2021 Pew Research Center study found that 63 percent of all Americans, not just Catholics, have a positive impression of Francis—which, naturally, are poll numbers that any candidate for president in the next election would love to have. He has amassed 18.9 million Twitter followers in English and, in 2019, became the subject of the acclaimed film *The Two Popes*, a Netflix production that received three Oscar nominations.

Looking back, it seems clear that the new pope benefitted from several media dynamics. First, the tone of much coverage of Catholicism after Pope Benedict XVI's resignation announcement in mid-February 2013 had been unrelentingly gloom and doom: a Vatican in disarray, rank and file Catholics demoralized and outraged by the abuse crisis, unresolved financial scandals, and the ongoing exodus of people out of the Church in many parts of the developed world. Pope Benedict was often depicted as the poster boy for this malaise, an out-of-touch archconservative intellectual living in an ivory tower while his Church burns. After a month of that sort of negativity, reporters and commentators were eager for a more positive story to tell, and the new pope supplied it in droves.

Second, Pope Francis had the great fortune of coming into office without a narrative. Cardinal Joseph Ratzinger had been a public figure on the global scene for a quarter-century, and his narrative followed him into the papacy. Cardinal Jorge Mario Bergoglio of Buenos Aires, on the other hand, kept a remarkably low profile prior to his election to the papacy, remaining almost unknown even among his fellow Argentines. Indeed, so opaque was his profile that some observers, such as American Catholic writer George Weigel, actually made the mistake of assuming he was a theological conservative simply because he'd once fallen out of favor with his Jesuit superiors (forgetting that Jesuits fight over all kinds of things, not just politics) and because he'd been appointed by Pope John Paul II (forgetting that John Paul actually appointed plenty of liberals, including several of the American prelates of whom Weigel disapproved). Francis thus had the opportunity to create a new narrative of his own, and his early moves were unfailingly brilliant, from going back to the clerical residence where he'd stayed before the conclave to pay his own bill and pack his own bag, to refusing to live in the papal apartments and opting instead for the Casa Santa Marta, a sort of hotel on Vatican grounds built under Pope John Paul II. Never mind that his accommodations in the Santa Marta are actually far more comfortable, and certainly more functional, than in the apartments—they're less regal, and that's what mattered. By the time he was done, Francis had created an image for himself that an entire team of Madison Avenue marketing gurus might have dreamed up but probably would have been unable to deliver.

Third, Pope Francis was quickly perceived as a more "liberal" figure than the previous two popes, which gave him not only immediate support in one side of the Church's internal debates—after all, Benedict had that too—but the affection of much of the mainstream media establishment. It's not just that many reporters and editors are themselves fairly liberal and therefore inclined to like Francis; we're in the storytelling business, and a liberal maverick from the Third World shaking up the world's most legendarily stick-in-the-mud institution is just great drama.

Whatever the reasons, the fact of the matter is that Pope Francis early on became surrounded by an overwhelmingly positive narrative, which, to some extent, insulated him from criticism and skepticism, and which continues to do so to this day. That's an awesome asset for any public leader to have, and Francis continues to wield it on multiple fronts, from diplomatic initiatives aimed at conflict resolution and peacemaking to ecclesiastical efforts to promote stronger ties among the world's great religions, perhaps especially between Christianity and Islam.

THE ANTI-NARRATIVE

And yet.

And yet, from the beginning, the image of a smiling, laughing, loving, humble populist and maverick reformer was not the only narrative about the new pope. In other circles, a counternarrative began to form, beginning with the suggestion that the new pope had not been properly elected. Traditionalist Italian Catholic writer Antonio Socci gave voice to that view in his 2014 book *Non è Francesco*, "He Is Not Francis," arguing that Benedict's resignation was invalid canonically, so there never should have been a conclave in the first place, and that Francis' election violated the rules of the conclave because an extra blank ballot was discovered on the fourth round of voting but the results were not tossed out, meaning that even if a vacancy had existed, Francis wasn't actually elected. The end of that chain, naturally, was the insistence that Benedict XVI remained the true pope. The thesis was immediately discredited by pretty much everyone involved in the conclave, including the cardinals who elected Bergoglio, but the book nonetheless sold like hotcakes in some Catholic circles, and its core thesis remains a firm conviction among some Francis critics. (The appeal of the book lies in part in its subtitle, *La Chiesa nella Grande Tempesta*, "The Church in the Great Storm," invoking quasi-apocalyptic imagery about the damage Francis was causing to the faith.) While the main claim of the book, the illegitimacy of Francis' election, never gained much traction among mainstream conservative critics, it did bequeath one linguistic trope: among critics, it's still more common to refer to Francis as "Bergoglio," using his given name, than to call him "pope."

(There's an especially inane version of the "not really pope" theory, by the way, that holds that Bergoglio's election is somehow in doubt because a shadowy group of cardinals and other senior prelates known as the "Sankt Gallen Group" campaigned for him. However, if a pope's election is to be invalidated just because some group of cardinals urges others to vote for him, then we probably haven't had a validly elected pope for centuries, and, quite possibly, ever. The election of a pope is a political process, and cardinals are political animals as much as anybody else. Indeed, most regard this as the most important decision they'll make in their lives, and so of course they take it seriously, and sometimes share their reflections with others. If you think about it, the idea of a conclave as a semi-transcendent spiritual operation untinged by any human reality actually is more Gnostic than Catholic anyway.)

Among doubters who weren't quite ready to follow Socci, another narrative began to emerge about the new pope, this one with much more mainstream appeal. It holds that Francis is arrogant, capricious, and prone to abuse his authority and to disregard basic standards of human decency in his blind exercise of power. This narrative took a bit longer to form, but once it was in place, it metastasized quickly. In February 2017, anonymous posters cropped up in Rome depicting an angry-looking pope with this text: "Oh, Frankie, you've taken over congregations, removed priests, decapitated the Order of Malta and the Franciscans of the Immaculate Conception, ignored Cardinals. . . . But where's your mercy?" (Without going into details, it was more or less a catalogue of traditionalist and conservative complaints against Francis, set against his frequent use of "mercy" as a rhetorical trope and a standard for authentic Christianity.) One year after the posters, we got *Il Papa Dittatore*, "The Dictator Pope," by "Marcantonio Colonna," the pen name of a Jesuit-educated English writer named Henry Sire, who lived in Rome from 2013 to 2017. (The historical Marcantonio Colonna was the admiral of the papal fleet in the 1571 Battle of Lepanto, which was decisive in thwarting an Islamic conquest of Europe.)

The book delivers a searing indictment of Francis as a smiling, loving figure as long as the cameras are on, but behind the scenes "arrogant, dismissive of people, prodigal with bad language, and notorious for furious outbursts of temper which are known to everyone from cardinals to the chauffeurs." Based on largely unnamed sources within the Vatican, including cardinals, the author asserts that "Francis is showing that he is not the democratic, liberal ruler the cardinals thought they were electing in 2013, but a papal tyrant the likes of whom has not been seen for many centuries," accusing the Argentine pontiff of creating a "reign of fear" inside the Vatican and in wider circles in the Church.

On social media in traditionalist and conservative Catholic circles one can often find even worse fare, including suggestions that behind Francis' dictatorial reign lies demonic possession, sexual deviance, and much more.

All this, however, was merely prolegomena for the emergence of the real superstar of the Bergoglio counternarrative: Italian Archbishop Carlo Maria Viganò, who, in August 2018, on the eve of Pope Francis' trip to Ireland for a World Meeting of Families, dropped the ecclesiastical equivalent of a nuclear bomb. A former papal ambassador to the United States during the Obama administration, Viganò charged that he had informed Pope Francis in June 2013 of sexual abuse charges against Theodore McCarrick, at the time a cardinal and trusted papal advisor, but that Francis had done nothing, making him, effectively, part of the cover-up. Viganò demanded that Francis resign as a gesture of accountability.

Francis never directly responded to Viganò, restricting himself at one point to encouraging journalists to look into the charges and the man making them, saying, "You are capable enough as journalists to draw your own conclusions." From that point forward, Viganò began issuing one declaration after another, each seemingly more radical in its critique than the last. In 2020, in an interview with Italian journalist Marco Tosatti, Viganò asserted that Francis is guilty of heresy for the pontiff's promotion of pastoral outreach to gay, lesbian, and transgendered persons. "For Bergoglio and his entourage sodomy is not a sin that cries out for vengeance in the presence of God, as the Catechism teaches," Viganò said. "Bergoglio's words on this topic—and even more the actions and words of those who surround him—unfortunately confirm that an operation of legitimization of homosexuality is currently underway."

In all honesty, most mainstream observers had tuned out Viganò by that point, put off by his frequent ramblings about the machinations of a "New World Order." In March 2022, for example, Viganò issued a lengthy statement on the Russian invasion of Ukraine, which built toward a call for the West to stop opposing Russia and instead build an alliance with Moscow in a titanic struggle against what he called "the globalist techno-health transhuman monster." Nevertheless, in deeply conservative Catholic circles, including the most embittered critics of Pope Francis, Viganò remains a key point of reference. He's also expanded his reach into secular politics, becoming an enthusiastic supporter of former US President Donald Trump, whom Viganò described in an October 2020 open letter as "the one who opposes the deep state, the final assault of the children of darkness."

At a certain level, much of this could simply be seen as amusing, except for the impact it has on delegitimizing even fair critiques of the Francis papacy. By now, anyone attempting to offer such food for thought tends to get fired upon in social media circles by breathless enthusiasts of the pontiff shouting, "You're just part of the Viganò crowd!" (Ironically, Pope Francis got lucky not only in his narrative but also in his counternarrative, with a Critic-in-Chief so easy to write off.)

Returning to the more mainstream anti-Bergoglio narrative, beyond authoritarianism, another article in the indictment is that the pope is either an outright heretic or at least so casual about doctrine as to allow heresy in through the back door. While that charge circulated almost immediately in some limited circles, it gained a wider following with the issuance of the pontiff's 2016 apostolic constitution *Amoris Laetitia*, which opened a cautious door to reception of Communion by divorced and civilly remarried Catholics under certain conditions. Not only, in the eyes of critics, did that decision imperil core Catholic teachings on marriage and the Eucharist, but it also more or less repealed an earlier decision on the same subject by Pope John Paul II, thus outraging conservatives loyal to the Polish pope.

After 2016, it became increasingly common to hear open charges of Pope Francis taking a wrecking ball to the established teachings of the Church. For example, the presence of a statue of a female indigenous Amazonian deity called the "Pachamama" at a Synod of Bishops in 2019 triggered an avalanche of tweets, Facebook posts, and more, all decrying the New Age pantheistic relativism on display at Francis' summit. At one point during the tumult, I considered proposing a Catholic twist on Godwin's law, the well-known internet dictum that states that the first person to compare their opponent in an online argument to the Nazis loses. I wanted to suggest that the first person in any Catholic row to call his or her opponent a heretic loses, but, just as Godwin's law hasn't exactly diminished the number of Nazi analogies flying around social media—just look at the rhetoric Putin used to justify the Russian invasion of Ukraine—I didn't suppose my modest proposal would make much of a difference either.

In 2017, a group initially composed of sixty-two signatories released a document they chose to call, in Latin, *Correctio filialis de haeresibus propagatis*, which translates as "Filial correction of propagated heresies." In it, they accused Pope Francis of seven specific doctrinal errors—or, at least, of risking those errors through imprecise language and suspect policy decisions. These were the errors:

1. Saying that God's grace is not always enough to keep a person out of serious sin.
2. Admitting the possibility of civil divorce and remarriage, and subsequently living as if married, without the couple placing themselves in a state of mortal sin.
3. Espousing the ability to have full knowledge of a divine law, yet to voluntarily break it without placing oneself in a state of mortal sin.
4. Espousing the ability to sin against God by keeping a divine prohibition.

5. Admitting the possibility of morally sanctioned sexual acts within a civil marriage, when one or both parties are within a sacramental marriage to another.
6. Denial that some behaviors are objectively grave and unlawful.
7. Providing the Eucharist to individuals who are divorced and remarried, and offering forgiveness to divorced and remarried individuals even if they don't abandon their new partner.

Italian Monsignor Antonio Livi, a dogmatic theologian at Rome's Pontifical Lateran University—known, by the way, as "The Pope's University" because it's run by the Diocese of Rome and falls directly under papal authority, unlike other pontifical universities, which are entrusted to religious orders—summed up the spirit of the letter in a 2018 interview. "For more than fifty years heretical, evil theologians have tried to conquer power, and now they have succeeded," Livi said. "That is why I speak of heresy in power." Note that his critique isn't just of Francis but of every pope since Vatican II, including Benedict XVI, who Livi said "maintained an Orthodox and pious position in adoration of God and respect for the sacredness of the Incarnation, but in the end, [he] too was effectively united with these heretical theologians."

Honestly, though, Livi's rhetoric just scratches the surface of the number of fronts on which accusations of heresy against the pope get tossed around on social media channels and in the blogosphere. In early 2016, Fr. Dwight Longenecker, himself a prominent conservative Catholic writer, offered this round-up of the sort of thing that's routinely in the Catholic ether:

> Anne Barnhardt refers to Pope Francis as a "diabolical narcissist," and in an interview at Creative Minority Report calls the pope a "fag hag." The anonymous Mundabor, like most of the radical blogs, calls for *Amoris Laetitia* to be withdrawn and ponders how a heretical pope might be deposed, while Barnhardt, writing here at The Remnant, writes an incendiary and ludicrous article calling for "all bishops who are true Catholics" to rise up and depose Jorge Bergoglio. Meanwhile, the shadowy TradCatKnight deals not only in conspiracy theories about the apostasy of "Pope Bergoglio," but also warns of chem trails, the nefarious Jews, global government conspiracies, the skull and bones club and various other ominously apocalyptic stories. Novus Ordo Watch chronicles the diabolical machinations of the post–Vatican II church, the invalid resignation of Pope Benedict XVI, church conspiracies and lies about Fatima and the widespread apostasy in the highest levels of the Vatican.

That, needless to say, is no more than a random sample of a much larger phenomenon.

Third and finally, it's also become a fixed point in the Bergoglio counternarrative that history's first pope from Latin America is a socialist, someone who cozies up to radical Latin American strongmen such as Evo Morales of Bolivia and Nicolás Maduro of Venezuela, someone who doesn't believe in free markets or trade and supports government solutions to virtually all problems, and, perhaps above all, someone who hates the United States of America and everything it stands for. Needless to say, while you can find adherents of this view of Pope Francis most places, they tend to be especially concentrated in conservative circles in the States.

DECONSTRUCTING THE NARRATIVE

To sum up, aside from ongoing doubts regarding the legitimacy of his election in some fringe circles, the main elements of the anti-Bergoglio counternarrative are the following: (1) Bergoglio is a dictator; (2) Bergoglio is a heretic; (3) Bergoglio is a socialist.

To be clear, it's not just hotheaded Catholics with too much time and too many social media platforms on their hands who recycle these charges. I have heard them, in exactly those words, from cardinals, bishops, and extremely senior lay officials in the Church, as has anyone else who covers this beat. They may represent a distinct minority in terms of broader Catholic and public opinion, where the positive narrative about Pope Francis still reigns supreme. Nonetheless, some of the people who voice these views are influential figures within the Church, and there's no doubt the drumbeat of criticism has weakened Pope Francis' leadership in some areas and made it more difficult for him to garner the benefit of the doubt in some quarters.

Yet a moment's reflection is enough to conclude that while each charge may contain a grain of truth, as stated it's wildly exaggerated, and the fact that rational people could think these things probably says more about the way contempt distorts perceptions in the twenty-first century than it does about the pope.

Let's begin with the "dictator pope" accusation. On the face of it, it's an odd charge to level against a pope, since Church law invests him with what's called "supreme, full, immediate, and universal ordinary power in the church," which, the law states, "he is always able to exercise freely." In other words, when it comes to governing the Catholic Church, a pope is basically an absolute monarch by definition, and whether he's a benign monarch or not thus rests in the eyes of the beholder. Moreover, Bergoglio didn't seize these powers in some sort of violent coup; he was elected by his fellow cardinals and immediately acknowledged as the new sovereign by his predecessor, Benedict XVI. Granted, some modern popes have been more enthusiastic about wielding those powers than others, but it seems a bit disingenuous to accuse Francis of doing little more than exercising the authority the law of the Church affords him.

A related irony, by the way, is that Pope Benedict XVI was often accused of being a negligent manager, and it was said the Church needed a pope who would take the reins of governance more firmly in his own hands. For a decade, Pope Francis has been doing precisely that, and, for his trouble, he's accused of being a madcap tyrant—all of which probably belongs in the "it's not easy being pope" file.

To be sure, there's an entirely legitimate conversation to be had about whether Pope Francis has always exercised the considerable powers he enjoys wisely, prudently, or humanely. To take one example, Francis issued legal decrees known as "rescripts" at the start of an investigation into financial crime in 2019 that led to the indictment and trial of ten defendants, including, for the first time, a prince of the Church, Italian Cardinal Giovanni Becciu, for their roles in a $400 million land deal in London that went bad. The pope's rescripts authorized Vatican prosecutors to carry on an investigation in secret, thus not affording the targets a chance to present exculpatory evidence before indictment, as well as allowing essentially unlimited electronic surveillance and the physical detention of both persons and assets, without any possibility of judicial review. While judges in the Vatican tribunal eventually ruled that the pope did not exceed his authority in issuing those rescripts, that's only because Church law makes him both the supreme executive and judicial power. Whether the rescripts were consistent with due process and accepted international legal standards is another matter entirely, and raising the question is not, ipso facto, to participate in the culture of contempt.

There's a big gap between that sort of reasoned discussion about particular decisions, however, and sweeping charges of autocracy. It's especially offensive in the case of Pope Francis, because one would do well to remember that he knows in his bones what a real dictatorship is like, having lived through Argentina's "Dirty War" and having taken considerable risks in sheltering some dissidents from the regime. Moreover, no pope in modern times has put such great stress on the idea of "synodality," meaning making decisions on the basis of widespread consultation. Granted, critics sometimes think this consultation is a sham intended to provide a veneer of legitimacy to predetermined conclusions, sort of like plebiscites in the old Soviet Union. Still, relatively few actual dictators go to such lengths to give ordinary people a voice, no matter what eventually happens with their input.

It's also worth saying that the charge that a pope is a "dictator" is one of the more time-honored weapons in the rhetorical arsenal of Catholic dissenters of all sorts. Pope Pius X, for instance, now a saint of the Catholic Church, was characterized as a "dictator" for imposing loyalty oaths on clergy and creating watchdog groups, known as "sodalities," to root out alleged "modernists" who were seen as secularizing the Catholic faith. John Paul II, also now canonized as a saint, was accused of being a "dictator" by liberal critics for clamping down on progressive theologians, imposing new leadership on the Jesuit order, centralizing control of some matters in the Church such as liturgical translation, and issuing a universal catechism to replace regional and local compendiums of Church teaching. Even "Good Pope John," St. John XXIII, was sometimes seen as an autocrat for imposing an ecumenical council on the Church that no one at the time had ever really requested. The point is that opponents of a given pope often style him as a dictator running roughshod over legitimate dissent, while supporters generally complain that he's not moving far enough or fast enough and, if anything, urge him to be even more aggressive in exercising his powers to implement his vision. There's nothing new under the sun, in that sense, except the ubiquity of cheap speech that allows this old canard to take on new life in the cybersphere.

The second element of the Bergoglio counternarrative, that Francis is a heretic, is, if anything, even sillier. To begin with, heresy in its classic form is a denial of some element of the creeds that form the basis of orthodox Christian faith—for instance, that Christ is divine, that God is a Trinity of persons, that Jesus physically rose from the dead, or that the Church is one, holy, catholic, and apostolic. In that sense, Francis is obviously no heretic, as he recites those creeds every time he celebrates Sunday Mass and has never done or said anything to call them into question.

What people usually mean when they call Francis a heretic, therefore, is that his allegedly sloppy language or dubious practices cause confusion about the faith. For example, the dust-up over the Pachamama incident at the Amazon Synod wasn't that Pope Francis explicitly advocated pantheism, but rather that his indulgent and naïve desire to accommodate the sensibilities of indigenous persons sent mixed messages. The debate over *Amoris Laetitia* ran the closest to a real charge of teaching heresy, but even there the indictment generally is that Francis indirectly undercut orthodox doctrine on the sanctity and indissolubility of marriage, not that he directly repealed that doctrine. The same point applies to the oft-repeated charge among more militant members of the pro-life movement that Pope Francis isn't sufficiently firm on abortion, including not supporting Communion bans for pro-choice politicians. That, too, amounts to a judgment call rather than a doctrinal formula. In other words, the debate isn't so much over his orthodoxy, but rather his judgment—and, even if that judgment were to be found wanting in multiple cases, it still wouldn't make him a heretic.

(By the way, let's also pause and note the irony that the same people who accuse Francis today of heresy often leveled the same accusation against dissenters from Pope John Paul II—and, many times, it was because they dared question his exercise of papal power. Back then, it was common to hear the assertion that a strong papacy is the bedrock of the Catholic Church, and those who seek to dilute papal authority, for instance by promoting "collegiality," or shared decision-making, were simply naïve about the need for a strong center of authority in Rome to hold the line in a secularized world. In other words, Francis critics are sometimes guilty of historical amnesia, forgetting that the same papal traits that were the foundation of orthodoxy in their view just twenty years ago are now being lampooned as a heretical reign of terror.)

Finally, there's Pope Francis as a socialist. In reality, anyone who has undertaken a serious study of Pope Francis' political philosophy will tell you that it's best expressed as a form of "Peronism," the political thought associated with Juan Perón in his native Argentina. While almost impossible to express in a set of bullet points, Peronism is usually defined as a vague blend of populism and nationalism that contains within itself many different currents. Whatever it is, Peronism is not premised on the classic tenets of socialism, meaning state ownership of the means of production, distribution, and exchange. Indeed, Perón understood his political movement as a third way between capitalism and communism, with the state taking on the role of mediator between management and labor but not of owner and operator.

By "socialist," of course, people usually just mean "liberal," meaning that Pope Francis supports a robust role for public intervention in the economy and other areas of life, including in poverty relief, environmental protection efforts, the provision of health care and education, and a host of other areas. Naturally, there's plenty of room for debate on such things, but there's a key point often overlooked in the "Francis the socialist" drumbeat: if Pope Francis is a socialist for holding those convictions, then so is every pope of the modern era, not to mention the *Catechism of the Catholic Church*. John Paul II supported a universal human right to health care, for instance, and Pope Benedict was so insistent about the need for stronger environmental protections that he was actually dubbed "the Green Pope." (Among other things, Benedict had solar panels installed atop the roof of the Vatican's Paul VI Audience Hall and signed deals for the replanting of European forests sufficient to make the Vatican officially carbon-neutral.)

In general, Catholic social teaching is open to seeing certain social goods, such as clean water, health care, and a decent standard of living, as "rights"—more so than much conservative Anglo-Saxon political theory, which tends to see only personal freedoms as "rights" that the state has a duty to guarantee. In that sense, Pope Francis' social agenda, believe it or not, actually turns out to be one of the least innovative elements of his papacy. On almost every front, Francis is either just repeating what was already there, for instance his rhetoric on war, or undertaking a logical development on trajectories already in motion, such as his declaration of capital punishment as "inadmissible." Logically speaking, to call this pope a "socialist" is to cherry-pick, because one could just as easily say the same thing of the Catholic Church and its leadership writ large, if such is the standard.

BERGOGLIO AND CONTEMPT

To repeat the point, just as with Pope Benedict XVI, there is vast terrain for debate and criticism about the Francis papacy. Even strictly by-the-book Catholics are only required to believe that the pope is infallible on a very narrow canon of issues directly related to faith and morals, which certainly does not extend to which orders he chooses to suppress or encourage, which priests he removes and which he promotes, or which cardinals he chooses to ignore. On the matter of Francis' exercise of power, for example, there are many moderates in Church affairs who see it as a bit excessive.

There's a world of difference, however, between posing such entirely legitimate criticisms of a papacy and suggesting that the pope himself is illegitimately elected, promoting heresy, or so drunk with power that he's effectively Vladimir Putin in a cassock. Those accusations, which are remarkably frequent in some circles, reflect a spirit of contempt for the person as well as the policies, and are aided in their circulation by the era of cheap information in which the world, and therefore the Church, finds itself.

CHAPTER SIX

Case Study: The Archbishop Who Supposedly Wanted Pope Francis to Die

Even though it was less than a decade ago, it's still hard for many Catholics to remember the charged climate that existed in the Church in the fall of 2015, when Pope Francis had just wrapped up his second Synod of Bishops on the Family, setting the stage for his ultra-controversial apostolic exhortation *Amoris Laetitia* in early 2016. The dominant issues during the two synods had been the question of whether divorced and civilly remarried Catholics, who were technically barred from the sacraments due to the sin of adultery, could be readmitted under certain conditions with the guidance of a priest and, ultimately, the local bishop. Because such a move was perceived by critics as a direct repudiation of the teaching of the late Pope John Paul II on the subject, it forced the battle lines in the Church to be drawn squarely between conservatives who saw Pope Francis as rejecting the legacy of his predecessors and progressives who saw Francis as reviving the reforming spirit of the Second Vatican Council (1962–65) that they believed had been stalled under John Paul II and Benedict XVI.

The debates over the issue during the two synods were intense, but outside the synod hall the rhetoric was even more heated and partisan, fueling speculation at the time that a formal schism in the Church between conservatives and progressives might be in the offing. In media circles, the hunt was on to identify the Blues and the Grays—meaning, in American idiom, who was on which side, especially among the bishops. Such taxonomy was inspired by the perception that the two synods had revealed a clear division between prelates who backed the reforming agenda of the new pope and conservatives nostalgic for the ancien régime who were ferociously opposed to it. The narrative of conservative opposition to Pope Francis within the Catholic hierarchy, which had been simmering in the background since his election in March 2013, erupted into full public view as a result of the two synods. It's worth remembering that after the first Synod on the Family in 2014, a respected English conservative Catholic journalist named Edward Pentin wrote a widely read book titled *The Rigging of a Vatican Synod?: An Investigation into Alleged Manipulation at the Extraordinary Synod on the Family*, which suggested that progressive forces at the first meeting had manipulated the system to produce their desired outcomes, riding roughshod over voices of dissent. Pentin's material in the book largely collected what was being said by more conservative bishops at the time, both out loud and sotto voce, about what they saw as Pope Francis steering the assemblies toward a predetermined outcome. This seemed to some to be a preemptive effort to delegitimize the pope's eventual decision before it even arrived. Looking back, it now seems clear that those two synods basically set the fault lines of the Pope Francis era into cement, defining both the opposition and the support in ways that have marked the rest of his papacy.

With that kindling already smoldering, on November 25, 2015, the left-of-center Italian newspaper *Il Fatto Quotidiano* (The Daily Fact) set off a blaze that was never really extinguished, with a sensational bombshell story claiming that a well-known conservative Italian archbishop, linked to the Communion and Liberation movement known to have been favored by Pope Emeritus Benedict XVI, had more or less publicly expressed a desire for Pope Francis to die. The headline was "Papa Francesco, il vescovo ciellino di Ferrara: 'Bergoglio deve fare la fine dell'altro Pontefice,'" which translates as "Pope Francis and the Communion and Liberation bishop of Ferrara: 'Bergoglio needs to end up like the other pontiff,'" a thinly veiled reference to Pope John Paul I, who died after just thirty-three days in office. Note the use of quotation marks in the original headline, which suggests that the words reported amounted to a direct quote from the prelate in question.

That prelate was Archbishop Luigi Negri of Ferrara-Comacchio, which lies in the northern Italian region of Emilia-Romagna near Bologna. Negri had been named to head that diocese by Benedict XVI in 2012, and, at the time, many observers of the Italian ecclesiastical scene thought the move may have set up Negri eventually to replace Cardinal Angelo Scola in the preeminent Italian see of Milan (Negri was born and raised in Milan), or perhaps Cardinal Carlo Caffarra in the equally prestigious Archdiocese of Bologna, as both Scola and Caffarra were seen as fellow conservatives. While the transition in the papacy in March 2013 rendered either of those outcomes improbable anyway, the scandal that erupted around Negri's alleged comments on Pope Francis essentially ended his ecclesiastical career, and he died on New Year's Eve 2021 essentially a footnote in recent Church history.

What's notable about all this is that *Il Fatto Quotidiano* never identified the sources who allegedly overheard Negri's remarks, which were supposedly made on a train ride in a private conversation with a priest of his diocese, and the paper made only a negligible effort to obtain comment from Negri before they went to print. Despite Negri's repeated denials, the storyline stuck because it fit the larger narrative of the day, which was that conservative prelates such as Negri were not only trying to obstruct the Pope Francis agenda but actually wanted him gone. That, in the end, is what makes the Negri episode a compelling example of the culture of contempt: it didn't matter what he actually said or thought, because he was a useful foil to advance a broader agenda. In this case, it wasn't originally the Catholic media that started the contretemps, since *Il Fatto Quotidiano* is a mainstream secular paper, but, as we've seen, in Italy such distinctions are always relative, and, in any event, the Catholic press gleefully picked up on the story as soon as it broke.

To this day, it's not clear what was actually said on that fateful train ride of October 28, 2015. What is clear, however, is that in the culture of contempt in today's media, that question—what really happened—is considered distracting at best, and, at worst, a betrayal of which side you're really on. The fact that trying to get to the truth of a situation is today considered an ideological maneuver—not by everyone, certainly, but by many of the shapers of culture—probably says everything that needs to be said about the situation we're in.

BACKGROUND

Luigi Negri was born in Milan in November 1941, and, as an adolescent, he attended a *liceo* (what Americans would call a high school) named for Giovanni Berchet, an Italian poet of the nineteenth century. While there, Negri met a young Italian priest and teacher named Fr. Luigi Giussani, who, at the time, was just launching a new group called Gioventù Studentesca, "Student Youth," aimed at bringing school students into a more active practice of their faith. From that point forward, Negri became a stalwart disciple of Giussani, whose guiding idea was that at the heart of the Christian faith is what he called an "event," meaning an encounter with Christ, which, Giussani argued, occurs in the context of the Church. During the student rebellions that swept European universities in 1968, Giussani's followers rejected the embrace of leftist causes that defined much student activism, and the result was the foundation of a new movement that came to be known as Communion and Liberation. The movement, which Giussani led until his death in 2005, became highly successful in attracting not only young people but also adults, including many personalities involved in the worlds of finance and politics, above all in Italy. Through it all, Negri was at Giussani's side, serving as the first diocesan president of the new Communion and Liberation movement in Milan from 1965 to 1967, and then, after his ordination to the priesthood in 1972, becoming a member of the international council of Communion and Liberation. He also played a key role in organizing the initial annual meetings of Communion and Liberation in 1975 and 1976, which became a premier event on the Italian calendar every year. In effect, Negri was seen as Giussani's "right hand man" among his most important supporters and aides.

Though Giussani himself was an intellectual and never sought any particular ideological affiliation, sociologically Communion and Liberation came to represent a conservative alternative to what was considered the liberal leadership of the Archdiocese of Milan under Jesuit Cardinal Carlo Maria Martini from 1980 to 2004. For years Martini was considered the "great white hope," the leading papal contender for the Church's liberal wing, while Giussani and his Communion and Liberation movement were seen as Martini's in-house conservative opposition. Things came to a head in 1995 when a member and former spokesman for Communion and Liberation, Roberto Formigoni, was elected president of the Lombardy region, which includes Milan, setting up a perceived showdown between a conservative Communion and Liberation political leader and a liberal ecclesiastical titan.

In that context, Negri was perceived as a Formigoni ally and a Martini opponent. Like Formigoni, he was perceived as a supporter of Italy's flamboyant former Prime Minister Silvio Berlusconi, despite the moral scandals surrounding Berlusconi that outraged a significant cross-section of Italian Catholic opinion. In terms of widely quoted public comments, Negri was also perceived as a staunch opponent of abortion, once famously blaming Italy's economic woes on the fact that "six million Italians were never born" after the legalization of abortion in 1978. Negri argued that a "scarcity of children," including Italy's notoriously low birth rate, had positioned the country for economic collapse. In another instance, Negri once said that he would deny Communion to center-left Catholic politicians who supported the push for a civil unions law in Italy that would regularize the situation of same-sex couples. The law authorizing civil unions was eventually approved in 2016.

Negri was first named a bishop in 2005 under the late Pope John Paul II, assigned to lead the relatively small Diocese of San Marino-Montefeltro in the Emilia-Romagna region. Just three months after his appointment, Negri launched a John Paul II International Foundation for the Social Magisterium of the Church in San Marino, devoted to supporting systematic study of the social teaching of the Polish pope. The project obviously enjoyed the favor of the powers that were in the Vatican at the time; among other things, Benedict XVI decided to make a pastoral visit to San Marino-Montefeltro in 2011, and, in 2012, Benedict made Negri a personal appointee to a Synod of Bishops he'd called in Rome devoted to the topic of the New Evangelization, a theme associated with the thinking of Giussani. Indeed, so close was Benedict's affection for Communion and Liberation that when Giussani died in 2005, then-Cardinal Joseph Ratzinger volunteered to lead his funeral Mass, and members of a female branch of Communion and Liberation known as Memores Domini ran Benedict's personal household both as a cardinal and later as pope.

As noted above, Negri was named the new Archbishop of Ferrara-Comacchio in December 2012, just three months before Benedict XVI would announce his resignation from the papacy. Negri took possession of the archdiocese on March 3, 2013, just ten days before the election of Pope Francis. He quickly established a reputation as an influential conservative in the Italian hierarchy. Among other things, he was the lone Italian bishop to order that the bells of all churches in the archdiocese should sound in August 2015 to recall the Christian martyrs of Mosul in Iraq, who had been killed during the ISIS onslaught in the traditionally Christian Nineveh Plains areas in the northern region of the country.

What all that meant was that by the time the *Il Fatto Quotidiano* story appeared in November 2015, Negri was ideally positioned in Italian public opinion to be cast in the role of a Pope Francis opponent: an outspoken conservative, linked to a movement known to have been favored by Francis' more conservative predecessors, and with a profile all his own as a prelate whose own theological and political orientation were at odds with the new winds blowing in the Pope Francis era.

THE BOMBSHELL

As it happens, the story that cast Negri forever as the Italian bête noire of the Francis papacy actually was quite short—526 words in total, under the byline of Italian journalist Loris Mazzetti, a storied reporter known as a friend and collaborator of Enzo Biagi, a liberal Italian commentator who was forced out of his

position as a TV presenter on the Italian public broadcasting system RAI (*Radiotelevisione italiana*) during the
Berlusconi administration. Because it's important, here's
the full text of Mazzetti's report.

Pope Francis and the Communion and Libera-
tion bishop of Ferrara: "Bergoglio needs to end
up like the other pontiff"

*"Let's hope that with Bergoglio the Madonna makes
the same miracle as with the other." The reference
to Pope Luciani is thinly veiled. The phrase is of the
Archbishop of Ferrara, Luigi Negri, a leading prelate
in deep disagreement with Francis and a point of
reference of Communion and Liberation.*

*Negri, a student of Don Giussani, is also known for
having disagreed with the legal system when it charged
Berlusconi for the Ruby case. To those who said that
a great part of the Catholic world was upset by the
situation, he replied: "Indignation is not a Catholic
attitude."*

Against the appointment of priests of the street

*The motive of his disagreement: The recent nomina-
tions of Pope Francis to Bologna and Palermo, dioceses
for many years in the hands of Communion and
Liberation, to the bishops Matteo Zuppi and Corrado
Lorrefice, two priests of the streets.*

Monsignor Negri on October 28, on a train that left Roma-Termini (eyewitnesses have recounted what happened) gave free rein to his thinking in a loud voice, which appears to be his habit, unconcerned about the few others present in the first class cabin, with his secretary, a young priest with the kind of look that matters in ecclesiastical circles, with two cell phones ready to intercept the calls that came to the archbishop. "After the nominations to Bologna and Palermo," he blurts, *"even I could be the pope. It's a scandal. It's incredible, I have no words. I've never seen anything like it."*

The high prelate, ignoring the witnesses, wasn't content and had to talk with someone. He asked his secretary to call a longtime friend who was also from Communion and Liberation, Raffaele Farina, known as "Agent Betulla," adding to the intrigue. [Note: The reference was to an Italian politician and journalist believed to have a close relationship with the country's Secret Service.] *Still not satisfied, Negri continued to say to the young priest: "These are appointments made with a complete disregard of the rules, with a method that doesn't respect anyone or anything. The appointment to Bologna is incredible. I promised to Caffarra that I would show the green mice to that one* [an Italian idiom meaning, basically, to reveal the true colors of someone], *not letting even one thing pass during a meeting. The other appointment in Palermo is even*

*more serious. That one [Lorefice] wrote a book about
the poor—what does he know about the poor?—and
about Lercaro and Dossetti, his role models, and two
of those who have ruined the Italian church."* [Note:
Cardinal Giacomo Lercaro and Father Giuseppe
Dossetti, both deceased, are considered heroes of
progressive Italian Catholicism.]

The conference and the belly of the curia

Yesterday, Il Fatto *tried to contact Archbishop Negri
to ask if he wanted to clarify his words. "Yes, I believe
he was on that train on Oct. 28," said his spokesman,
Father Massimo Manservigi, listening to the quotes
we repeated to him. "But right now [it was 9:30 p.m.]
the bishop is giving a talk at the university and it's not
possible to contact him."* Il Fatto *is ready to hear any
eventual explanations by the prelate.*

*In any event, it's difficult to believe that Monsignor
Negri spoke only in his own name without revealing a
state of mind shared by the Vatican caste. If Bergoglio
wants, as he's promised, to fulfill the promise of Pope
John XXIII of a "church of the people of God," he'll
have to drive out the merchants from the temple.*

In its online edition the next day, *Il Fatto Quotidiano* added a postscript.

Reached by the editor of Nuova Ferrara, *Stefano Scan-
sani, after the Mass of Nov. 25, Monsignor Negri did*

not issue a denial. [Note: *Nuova Ferrara* is the local newspaper in what was then Negri's archdiocese.] *The archbishop said he'd react to the article in the next few hours, and added: "Did someone record it? This new episode explains a lot about the theological hatred against the church."*

Several points about the report are important to note. First, the "eyewitnesses" who allegedly overheard Negri's remarks are not identified in the piece, and they were never named as the controversy unfolded. Second, the quotations attributed to Negri are highly detailed, presented as verbatim accounts of what he said during that train ride of October 28, 2015, even though there apparently was no recording of the conversation, since neither *Il Fatto Quotidiano* nor any other media outlet ever presented one. Third, the newspaper by its own account approached a spokesman for Negri for comment on such an explosive story only at 9:30 p.m. the night before going to press the next morning, which all but assured there would be little chance for Negri to comment before the article appeared. Fourth, the article includes a few literary flourishes seemingly intended more for dramatic purposes than straightforward reporting, including describing the young priest traveling with Negri as having "the kind of look that matters in ecclesiastical circles." Fifth, the reporter also asserts, without providing any support for the claim, that Negri was speaking for an entire "Vatican caste" in his alleged complaints about Pope Francis.

In sum, the original November 25 story had enough dubious elements that it might, under other circumstances, have been written off by most readers as little more than idle gossip. Falling as it did precisely in a moment in which a powerful new narrative about the Catholic Church in the Pope Francis era was taking shape, however, such critical instincts were largely brushed aside in the rush to take sides either for or against what Negri had been reported to have said. The working assumption seemed to be that if Negri hadn't actually said these things out loud, he probably thought them—and if he didn't, others certainly did. More troublingly, Catholic media outlets and blogs, both in Italy and around the world, largely fed on the frenzy, generally taking it for granted that Negri had actually said what was quoted and proceeding to argue either for or (mostly) against the sentiments expressed.

As noted above, Negri never denied having been on the train in question. In later comments on the supposedly overheard conversation, he conceded that he probably did make some negative comments about the appointments of Zuppi and Lorefice, though not in a personal key, but rather in terms of broader cultural questions about the state of the Italian Church. He also acknowledged that he may have said something about Pope Francis but insisted that he was not referring to the 1978 death of Pope John Paul I. Instead, he said, if he said something about the Madonna, he was referring to the assassination attempt on Pope John Paul II on May 13, 1981. The Polish pope always attributed his survival that day to the intervention of the Madonna, noting that it was the feast day of Our Lady of Fatima, believing that Mary had caused the flight path of would-be assassin Mehmet Ali Ağca's bullet to deviate and save his life. Negri said he often called upon the Madonna to protect popes in light of that incident, so if he invoked the Madonna in that conversation, it was to pray for the pope's safety and not his demise. Such initial confusion about what he may have said is understandable, given that in the overcharged atmosphere of October 2015, this was probably just one of hundreds of conversations Negri had with various parties about what was going on in those days.

"What's clear," Negri said, "is that *Il Fatto* put its own interpretation of my thoughts in quotation marks, thus crucifying me with a phrase that I never uttered."

Later on, Negri would also acknowledge a mistake in not having issued a clearer denial of the story immediately, saying he worked out his response with Caffarra, a fellow conservative, who advised him that his accountability wasn't to the press but to his people. Negri also said the episode illustrated what he called "the terrible force of anti-Christianity," which, he said, has a name: "Masonry." (For the record, there's no evidence that professed Masons were involved in the affair.)

REACTION AND FALLOUT

Though Negri may not have commented for the original report in *Il Fatto Quotidiano*, he did respond quickly, and emphatically, as the story gathered force. In one of his more memorable reactions, Negri insisted that the article was based on "inventions" so fantastic that the author needed "treatment for neuro-delusions," and he threatened legal action for defamation of character. Negri also said that he had requested an audience with Pope Francis to clarify the situation and to apologize for the scandal that had been created, noting that just two months before, he had publicly praised the pontiff's decision to stage a special Holy Year of Mercy from December 8, 2015, the Feast of the Immaculate Conception, to November 20, 2016, the Feast of Christ the King. Negri had said at the time that the decision to call the jubilee had caused him to feel an "increase in gratitude" toward Pope Francis. A year later, Negri told his hometown newspaper in Ferrara that he had sent a "long and detailed" account of the alleged conversation to Francis, and that Cardinal Pietro Parolin, the pope's Secretary of State, had informed him that the pope appreciated the document and had decided to grant the audience Negri had requested. However, if that session did ever take place, neither side ever disclosed it publicly before Negri's death in January 2022 at the age of eighty.

One especially painful aspect of the affair for Negri was the rupture it caused between him and the Communion and Liberation movement, which he had served all his life from his roots as an early follower of Don Luigi Giussani. At the time, many of the so-called "new movements" in the Catholic Church, which had enjoyed strong favor under Popes John Paul II and Benedict XVI, were suspected of harboring anti-Francis sentiments, and so the *ciellini*, as they're commonly called in Italy, felt the need to disassociate themselves from Negri as quickly and emphatically as possible. The movement issued a statement noting that Negri had not held any leadership position in Communion and Liberation since 2005, the year in which he was named the Bishop of San Marino-Montefeltro, and professing the movement's unwavering loyalty to "every gesture and word" of Pope Francis. Notably, no one in the movement ever claimed they couldn't imagine Negri saying the things he'd been quoted as having said.

In an interview a couple of months later, Negri acknowledged that the response of Communion and Liberation still rankled. "I told them they could at least have waited until some of my own comments came out before issuing that statement," he said. "Reading between the lines, it seemed to affirm that I might have said those things. Two months later they haven't changed a comma of that original version. Today, there's only one reality in Italy that believes this whole thing could have possibly happened: The movement to which I dedicated more than fifty years of my life."

Negri may have been overly optimistic that Communion and Liberation was the only party in Italy that swallowed the original *Il Fatto Quotidiano* story more or less whole. As late as March 2013, when Pope Francis was elected to the papacy, Negri was widely considered a leading contender to succeed Cardinal Angelo Scola in Milan, another alumnus of the Communion and Liberation movement. (Scola's resignation was eventually accepted in 2017, and he was replaced instead by Archbishop Mario Delpini, who had been an Auxiliary Bishop of Milan under Scola and his vicar general.) In truth, the possibility of Negri going to Milan almost certainly ended with the election of Pope Francis anyway, since Negri's brand of theological and political conservatism isn't quite what Francis looks for when naming bishops to important dioceses. However, Negri might have looked forward to a sort of elder statesman role, perhaps commenting on public affairs for various Italian media outlets, publishing articles and books, and giving high-level talks. Instead, the scandal set off by the *Il Fatto* piece made all that largely impossible. The only forces in the Church that seemed interested in Negri afterward were the deeply traditionalist and anti-Francis crowd, and Negri did develop some minor connections with it. In 2020, for instance, he signed an appeal asking that the COVID pandemic not be used as a pretext for restricting religious freedom; that appeal was being promoted by Italian Archbishop Carlo Maria Viganò, the former papal ambassador to the United States who infamously accused Pope Francis of covering up abuse committed by former Cardinal Theodore McCarrick, and who's gone to become public enemy number one of the Francis papacy. However, for the most part Negri stayed out of public polemics in retirement, always insisting on what he claimed was his personal philosophy: "One neither contests nor adulates a pope; one follows him."

Despite all that, when Negri died in January 2022, his supposed death wish for Pope Francis nevertheless framed the lead of every obituary in Italy and around the world, and, in virtually every case, it was taken for granted that he'd actually issued the direct quotations attributed to him in that original article from November 2015. If noted at all, his repeated denials were largely brushed off amid a rehearsal of his conservative credentials.

His funeral Mass was celebrated in Ferrara on January 5, 2022—led, by the way, by Zuppi, who was then president of the bishops' conference of Emilia-Romagna, the region that includes both Bologna and Ferrara, and who is today widely considered a leading candidate to replace Pope Francis with a similar agenda. That day, an old friend of Negri, an Italian politician and columnist named Renato Farina, asked this provocative question about his fellow journalists: "Monsignor Negri is lying there, inert and already blessed. So why are they still trying to kill him?"

Here's why the episode of Archbishop Luigi Negri qualifies as a chapter in the emergence of today's media-driven culture of contempt.

To begin with, let's assume for a moment, despite Negri's repeated and emphatic denials, that he actually said everything he was quoted as saying during that train ride with a priest friend in October 2015. By all accounts, it was clearly a private conversation, even if, according to the *Il Fatto* report, Negri spoke in a loud voice that could be overheard by other passengers. Ethically, there's still a question about the "gotcha journalism" involved in taking comments clearly not intended for public consumption and broadcasting them to the world in order to embarrass or discredit a public figure. We've all had the experience of saying things in private, to friends or family, we would not want to have shared with the rest of the world. Often, it's a matter of blowing off steam, saying things far more bluntly or harshly than we would if we knew we were being recorded for posterity. Often, the experience of getting those things off our chest helps calm us down and leads us to a more mature and balanced assessment. In Rome, my wife and I are blessed to have a large terrace in our apartment in the city, and quite often we have various

Catholic personalities over for lunches, dinners, and receptions. Almost to a person, they've all, and we along with them, said things in these private settings that none of us would ever want reported. Such intimate conversations are possible because of an atmosphere of trust. The benefit is that our gatherings usually attract a pretty wide cross-section of ecclesiastical outlooks, so people have the chance to hear dissenting reactions to their unvarnished impressions that may, in the long run, help frame their more considered opinions. What the *Il Fatto* piece effectively did was damage the possibility of any such trust, which, one could argue, is a disservice to the health of any society, including the Church.

(I realize, by the way, that this ship pretty much has sailed. Today, if a public figure is caught saying something untoward or controversial in any setting at all, no matter how private or intimate, it's considered fair game to make it public. However, I can recognize that reality without necessarily believing it's the best thing to do, either for journalism or for the health of civil society.)

The real point, however, is that we don't actually know what Negri said on that train ride. To this day, *Il Fatto Quotidiano* has never identified any of the alleged "oral witnesses" who claimed to have heard the comments, nor did they ever produce an audio recording or a transcript. Faced with Negri's repeated denials, neither *Il Fatto* nor most other media outlets, including those of a Catholic stamp, appeared to take them seriously.

When Negri died in early January 2022, this was the headline of the *Il Fatto* obituary: "Luigi Negri is dead, the Communion and Liberation archbishop who said: 'Let's hope that with Bergoglio, the Madonna works the same miracle as with the other one.'" In other words, it repeated its headline of seven years before, with no acknowledgment of Negri's various responses. More or less, that was the tenor of the coverage everywhere.

It's Journalism 101 that you never put anything in quotation marks that you're not absolutely sure the source in question actually said. If there's any doubt, you go to the source for clarification. So why was this elementary standard of tradecraft set aside in Negri's case? Most probably because a budding narrative about conservative opposition to a progressive pope was being shaped, and Negri's background and credentials made him an ideal choice to be cast in the role of implacable papal foe. Moreover, if his own movement was unwilling to stick its neck out to give him the benefit of the doubt, many journalists may have thought, then why should anyone else?

In other words, Negri presented a virtually irresistible magnet for the tensions swirling in the Catholic Church at the time, which have not abated today. Was Negri a deep conservative, clearly linked to the theological and political visions that dominated the John Paul II and Benedict XVI years? Certainly. Did he probably harbor private doubts and objections to much of the new course being charted by Pope Francis? I can't say for sure, because I never discussed it with him, but it certainly doesn't seem implausible. None of that, however, demonstrates with certainty that he actually said what he was quoted as saying, which was that he wanted the pope dead—and Negri went to his own death denying it.

This is one face of the culture of contempt: to take an individual person, in almost conscious disregard of the need to establish the truth, and to elevate that person into a lightning rod for broader political, cultural, and social tensions. All this goes on without any apparent regard for the consequences for the person involved, as if they're merely disposable raw material for the journalistic industry, whose finished product is designed to inflame public opinion and to fuel division because that's what sells. In the end, Archbishop Luigi Negri may well have been part of the episcopal opposition to Pope Francis, and, for all we know, might not have been terribly disappointed had the pontiff met an early end. What we know for sure, however, is that no one could ever prove that's what he wanted, and that treating it as Gospel fact anyway was an act of contempt, not just for Negri, but for what's supposed to be the *summum bonum* of the journalistic enterprise—that is, the truth.

CHAPTER SEVEN

Case Study: LifeSite

When observers of the Catholic media scene these days warn of increasing polarization and acrimony, when they decry the rise of a nasty edge seemingly premised on inflicting maximum harm on perceived enemies, when they lament the use of spin and "fake news" as weapons in ideological wars, they often have two media platforms above all in mind: Michael Voris' Church Militant and LifeSite News. Of the two, LifeSite generates greater online traffic and probably has the wider international reach, in part, perhaps, because it's been around longer; while Church Militant in its present form dates only to 2012, LifeSite was founded more than a quarter-century ago in 1997.

The LifeSite story is a fascinating one, in part because of the way it illustrates a basic truth about the culture of contempt: people who experience contempt from others often become fairly contemptuous themselves. As a corollary of the law of unintended consequences, this insight also suggests a rule of thumb about the best way to respond to a culture of contempt, which is to stop being contemptuous ourselves.

The story begins with the rise of the pro-life movement in Canada. Abortion under any circumstances was illegal in Canada until 1969, when the government of liberal prime minister Pierre Trudeau, father of Canada's current prime minister Justin Trudeau, amended the Criminal Code to permit abortion if a pregnancy threatened the health or life of a woman. At that point, Canadians opposed to abortion began to fear a trend toward wider liberalization. In the two decades that followed the 1969 move under Trudeau, a vigorous abortion debate arose in Canada that witnessed, among other things, the creation of an anti-abortion political lobby called the Campaign Life Coalition based in Hamilton, Ontario.

By the early 1990s, abortion had already been legalized in Canada, but the coalition continued its work pushing the pro-life case, as well as expanding into other issues such as euthanasia, stem cell research, same-sex marriage, gender identity, and artificial reproduction, in each case attempting to defend socially conservative values in an increasingly secular Canadian milieu. It was during this time that a young, newly fervent Catholic named John-Henry Westen began selling subscriptions for a pro-life newsletter called *Interim*, and later researching and writing reports on various issues for the coalition. Westen had grown up in a devout Catholic household and passed through a semi-atheistic phase in adolescence but began to reembrace the faith in earnest in his twenties. He attended the 1993 World Youth Day in Denver and began reading Catholic spiritual classics, including St. Louis Marie de Montfort's *True Devotion to Mary*. He also did a brief research project at the University of Florence and spent a week in Rome, an experience he would later describe as having a major impact in strengthening his budding faith.

In his new role at the coalition, Westen discovered a knack for communication. Angered by what he saw as the mainstream media's contemptuous treatment of pro-lifers and pro-life arguments, he began sending a daily digest of news items of interest and, from that, grew the foundation of LifeSite in 1997, which brought Westen together with a like-minded Canadian Catholic named Steve Jalsevac. Today it's no longer under the umbrella of the Campaign Life Coalition, although the two groups share some board members. Later, at a 2013 March for Life conference in Ottawa, Westen described the purpose of LifeSite as circumventing the mainstream media, insisting that traditional media platforms profoundly mislead the public through biased choices about what information to include, and to exclude, from their reports, and the only way around that bias is to build alternative channels of communication. In terms of its business model, LifeSite now consists of two separate nonprofit entities, one in Canada and one in the United States, and while it does take paid advertising, it relies for the bulk of its funds on small reader contributions and larger support from donors. LifeSite claims a global reach of 20 million people, and while it's not entirely clear what the basis for that number is, a certain degree of exaggeration about audience size is common practice in media companies. Cable channels, for instance, often tout the total number of households in which their programming is available, but not necessarily how many people are actually watching it. In 2018, tax returns filed by LifeSite reported an income of $1.6 million, mostly coming in the form of donor contributions.

So far, this would be a completely comprehensible exercise. There is no doubt that over the years many mainstream media outlets have provided scant coverage of the pro-life movement. In the United States, one focal point for this resentment is the annual March for Life in Washington, DC, held each year on the anniversary of the 1973 *Roe v. Wade* decision legalizing abortion. Despite generally freezing temperatures in January in Washington, tens of thousands of people—before COVID, in some cases, hundreds of thousands—turn out, making it the largest annual pro-life rally in the world. Yet from watching most nightly news programs in America, or scanning the front pages of American newspapers, you'd never know it happened. In programming segments on abortion debates, networks sometimes cast a reasoned, articulate pro-choice individual against a fulminating, angry pro-lifer, thereby stacking the deck before the conversation even starts. In those and many other ways, pro-lifers have a legitimate bone to pick with the media establishment, and their desire to build their own information systems is both natural and inevitable.

Beyond its coverage of pro-life issues, LifeSite has also ventured into other territory, becoming a leading platform for COVID skeptics, Pope Francis critics, and conservatives alarmed over the rise of an often ill-defined "New World Order." LifeSite often features, for example, the writings of Archbishop Carlo Maria Viganò, and the headline atop one such essay, published by LifeSite on March 7, 2022, is representative of much of the rest: "Globalists have fomented war in Ukraine to establish the tyranny of the New World Order," it asserts, followed by a subhead that reads, "The Ukrainian people, regardless of what ethnic group they may belong to, are merely the latest unwitting hostages of the supranational totalitarian regime that brought the national economies of the entire world to their knees through the COVID deception." In another celebrated instance, LifeSite published an essay by Westen in August 2021 examining the question of whether, by allowing a statue of the indigenous Amazonian deity Pachamama to be displayed at the Synod of Bishops on the Amazon in October 2019, Pope Francis bears a measure of responsibility for the divine chastisement represented by the COVID-19 pandemic. To illustrate the circles in which LifeSite content is promoted, in 2020 the website of the alt-right conspiracy group QAnon linked to LifeSite coverage of one of Viganò's missives.

Beyond its editorial policies, critics of LifeSite have also suggested that it sometimes plays fast and loose with reality and whips readers into a rage in order to boost traffic and increase contributions. In November 2019, LifeSite reported that Jesuit Fr. James Martin was under serious consideration to become the next Archbishop of Philadelphia, editorializing that, in tandem with Cardinals Blase Cupich in Chicago and Joseph Tobin in Newark, the addition of Martin would "establish a powerful cabal to force the normalization of homosexuality and transgenderism within the Catholic Church in the United States." To make things even more sensational, they ran the article along with a picture of Martin from one of his many TV appearances flashing a hand gesture known as "the horns," which, depending on context, can imply devotion to Satan, cuckoldry, a love for heavy metal music, or support for the University of Texas football team, not to mention just simple playfulness. Outraged LifeSite readers flooded the papal embassy in Washington with phone calls, emails, and letters. The only difficulty with the narrative is that LifeSite never named its source for the original report, and, by all accounts, Martin was never under consideration for Philadelphia, which went instead to Bishop Nelson Perez of Cleveland. In some circles, there was a suspicion that LifeSite had ginned up the "Martin to Philly" story knowing full well the sort of reaction it would generate, which would be good for business.

Detractors of LifeSite—and there are many—generally describe it as sensationalistic, misleading, highly partisan, and shrill to the point of being divisive.

ATTACK JOURNALISM

From its foundation, LifeSite also began to develop a different personality from other Catholic media platforms, one that had a decidedly sharper edge. Not only did it publish material setting out the arguments for the pro-life cause, but it began to take on the role of an avenger, seeking out individuals in the Church it felt weren't sufficiently pro-life, or who were deemed untrustworthy for other reasons, and exposing them. This sort of attack-style journalism led to a lawsuit in 2011, when a Canadian priest and former member of the Canadian Parliament named Raymond Gravel sued LifeSite for Canadian $500,000 (about $390,000 US) in alleged damages for repeatedly calling him "pro-abortion." Gravel, who voted in favor of pro-choice positions in parliament, and who consistently espoused liberal Catholic views on issues such as same-sex rights (he acknowledged being gay himself in an interview before his death), insisted that he was pro-choice but not pro-abortion: "I am against abortion. I regard human life as sacred and abortion as always being a tragedy in our society. We must do everything in our power, while showing respect for those involved, to limit the number of abortions and promote life," Gravel said. In 2013, a Quebec court allowed the lawsuit to go to trial, but Gravel died the next year of lung cancer before the case could be adjudicated.

Ironically, although Gravel voted pro-choice, the abortion debate was not his main legislative priority. Rather, it was the care of senior citizens, which is also an article of Catholic social teaching, including improving their access to national income supplements. Ironically, too, when Gravel was ordered by the Vatican in 2008 to withdraw from politics, on the basis that it's inappropriate for a priest to hold elected office, he complied, choosing his priesthood over his political career.

Make no mistake: Gravel surrendered any expectation of privacy and exemption from criticism when he decided to go into politics, and, in principle, there's nothing wrong with a news organization putting a spotlight on his record. Moreover, there's also nothing wrong in principle with a news organization actively campaigning against public officials it believes to be corrupt, dangerous, or just wrong. There's a long and distinguished history of such advocacy journalism, from the barbed coverage in the *New York Times* and *Harper's Weekly*, including Thomas Nast's merciless cartoons, which helped bring down Tammany Hall and Boss Tweed, to Edward R. Murrow's campaign against Senator Joseph McCarthy in the 1950s, which effectively marked an end to anti-communist witch hunts during the Cold War.

Yet many observers of LifeSite's coverage of the Gravel story couldn't help feeling that whatever the merits of their objections to Gravel's political positions, the tone of much of it seemed nasty to the point of being vindictive, especially by the typically genteel standards of Canadian public discourse. At one stage, the site accused Gravel of making "heretical and anti-life statements," labeling him a "renegade priest," and frequently encouraged readers to inundate both Gravel's bishop and the papal embassy in Canada with complaints. Gravel would later cite those appeals in his lawsuit, arguing they led directly to the Vatican order to exit politics and also cost him a teaching position as a Bible instructor in his home diocese of Joliette in southwestern Quebec.

As in many instances of the culture of contempt, the issue with LifeSite's pursuit of the Gravel story wasn't the story itself, which was undeniably legitimate and of clear public interest. The issue was the manner in which it was pursued, which suggested a sort of "scorched earth" journalism in which basic concepts of fairness, balance, and careful use of language got tossed out the window in favor of destroying the village in order to save it. Granted, LifeSite arguably was doing no more than following the broad temper of the times in the media business, but some might wonder if a self-described "Catholic" media outlet should, somehow, be different.

Another celebrated instance of LifeSite's penchant for attack-style journalism came in its coverage of a plagiarism scandal surrounding Fr. Thomas Rosica, a well-known Canadian priest and member of the Basilian order who was the CEO of the 2002 edition of World Youth Day in Toronto, and afterward founded Salt + Light TV, which quickly became Canada's largest Catholic media platform, in 2003. In addition, Rosica served for a spell as a part-time English-speaking aide to the Vatican Press Office for Synods of Bishops and other special events, even if he was never quite a "Vatican spokesman" as he was frequently billed in media appearances, and he wrote and spoke widely on Catholic affairs.

In February 2019, a reporter for LifeSite named Dorothy Cummings McLean first reported that in a speech he delivered on February 8, 2019, at Cambridge University in the UK, Rosica had passed off large sections of the speech as his own that were actually lifted from other Catholic writers and thinkers, including American Cardinal Edwin O'Brien, Canadian theologian Gregory K. Hillis, American Jesuit columnist Fr. Thomas Reese, German Cardinal Walter Kasper, and American Jesuit writer Fr. James Martin. From that point, LifeSite began scouring virtually everything Rosica had ever written or said out loud, revealing a pattern of plagiarism in academic articles, essays, speeches, and op-eds dating back more than a decade. Subsequent reports on LifeSite—and there were many—documented all the instances of what amount to intellectual property crimes in great detail. It was also discovered that Rosica had falsified his academic credentials, claiming falsely in his official biography to have earned an advanced degree from the École Biblique et Archéologique Française de Jérusalem.

In 2020, it was revealed by a scholar working on a book about plagiarism that Rosica had also plagiarized sections of at least three texts he'd ghostwritten for Canadian Cardinal Marc Ouellet, prefect of the Vatican's powerful Congregation for Bishops. The researcher who uncovered the texts, Michael V. Dougherty of Ohio Dominican University, noted that in some cases, Rosica had apparently used material in Ouellet's texts from a different cardinal published a few weeks previously, which were also largely plagiarized. As Dougherty put it, "One finds herein the remarkably complex phenomenon of a plagiarist plagiarizing a plagiarizing text produced by a different plagiarist."

By June 2019, Rosica was compelled to resign from his post as the CEO of Salt + Light, after having been placed on administrative leave in March. He was also forced to issue a series of public apologies, saying at one point, "I ask forgiveness for errors in not properly acknowledging individuals and attributing sources in my writings," and at another, "I realize that I was not prudent nor vigilant with several of the texts that have surfaced, and I will be very vigilant with future texts and compositions. . . . I take full responsibility for my lack of oversight and do not place the blame on anyone else but myself." On the other hand, Rosica insisted the plagiarism was not deliberate, suggesting that it could have been the result of "cut and paste" errors, meaning he copied a chunk of text into his own writings or speeches without remembering to add proper attribution.

Although he continues to be occasionally quoted in the media on various Catholic topics, Rosica, as of this writing, is still mired in what Church wags call "ecclesiastical Siberia," not entrusted with any significant new assignment and largely doing what he can to stay out of the line of fire.

For sure, there was no problem with the content of the LifeSite reporting in the Rosica case. Rosica was unquestionably a public figure; for the record, he probably wielded much greater influence in Catholic life in Canada than the secretary general of the Canadian bishops' conference, and certainly enjoyed a far higher profile. In all honesty, Rosica has no one to blame for his downfall but himself. Had he never plagiarized—a plagiarism so extensive and pervasive that it suggests awareness of what he was doing—he probably would still be running Salt + Light today, and perhaps would have been on course to becoming a bishop someday.

Nonetheless, as in the Gravel case, it was the nastiness and seeming vindictiveness of the anti-Rosica campaign on LifeSite that left a sour taste in the mouths of some observers of the Catholic press scene. For one thing, it seemed clear that Rosica had been targeted in part because of his pro–Pope Francis stance, which conflicted with the site's editorial line. For another, there was also a patently obvious personal animus involved in the crusade against Rosica, as he had been a frequent critic of LifeSite. In a 2013 interview with Sirius XM's The Catholic Channel, operated by the Archdiocese of New York, Rosica had this to say:

> We have an agency in Canada functioning called LifeSite. It purports itself to be a news service for the areas and issues of life. I will say very publicly to those listening: it is not credible, it does not speak for the Church, it is not ethical, it is not honest. I encourage people to know that this is not an authentic instrument at the service of unity and at the service of the Church. It is causing division. . . . For the one-tenth of kernel of truth that they purport to uncover—and there is truth in what they do—nine-tenths is exaggeration. It is bombastic, it is derisive, and it is divisive.

Then came Rosica's key soundbite: "I think we have to be very clear and say that part of the work of Satan is to divide—to pit people against each other—and they are succeeding quite well." The undisguised glee that much LifeSite coverage seemed to exude about Rosica's fall from grace, therefore, couldn't help but seem to some observers as the settling of a personal grudge rather than simple public interest journalism.

What all this illustrates, perhaps, is that whatever you may think of them, LifeSite and media platforms like it matter. In the two instances examined here, LifeSite managed to drive one priest judged unacceptable out of politics and another into exile from his media career. Whether it's done so through aggressive reporting and strong commentary, as good media platforms have always aspired to do, or through personal smear campaigns and the politics of contempt, may (somewhat) be in the eye of the beholder, but its relevance is beyond dispute.

SANCTIONS

Despite the controversies it's spawned over the years, Catholic bishops both in Canada and in the United States have adopted a basically laissez-faire stance toward LifeSite, neither endorsing it nor, at least openly, condemning it. Behind the scenes, some bishops have pressed for an ecclesiastical sanction against the site, or at least a declaration that it does not represent the Catholic Church, but so far there's been no official statement along those lines. It's dubious that such an intervention would accomplish much, since courts have already ruled that the term "Catholic" is in the public domain and thus not subject to copyright protection, so the bishops have no power to force a site to stop describing itself in those terms. Moreover, given the worldview of most LifeSite readers and supporters that ecclesiastical officialdom is part of the problem, expressions of disapproval from officialdom likely would only serve to enhance LifeSite's credibility.

LifeSite has also come in for criticism among mainstream media monitoring organizations. In 2016, the mainstream fact-checking site Snopes described LifeSite as a "known purveyor of misleading information." Another site, Media Bias / Fact Check, founded by editor Dave Van Zandt, has assigned LifeSite a "low credibility" rating, assigning poor rankings to both its factual accuracy and editorial bias, and faulted it for "the promotion of conspiracy theories, pseudoscience, and many failed fact-checks." As a sort of indirect response to such assessments, LifeSite has published pieces suggesting that the rise of the "fact-checking" industry is another way in which social elites seek to control the public perception of reality, implying that terms such as "debunked" are actually "propaganda tools."

Finally, LifeSite has also faced sanctions on several social media platforms. Its Twitter account has been suspended four times since 2018, though one of those temporary shutdowns occurred in error. Twice, the account was suspended for violating Twitter policies against "targeted misgendering or deadnaming of transgender individuals" ("deadnaming" means referring to an individual by their birth name rather than using the new name adopted as part of a transgender transition), and once for violating policies against spreading COVID-19 misinformation. YouTube suspended LifeSite's channel in February 2021 for consistently providing misleading information on the COVID pandemic, violating the service's policies against "health misinformation." Facebook actually permanently banned LifeSite from the platform in May 2021, saying that the site spread "false information about COVID-19 that could contribute to physical harm." To date, however, none of these informal sanctions appears to have had much impact on LifeSite operations, fundraising, or audience size. As we'll see in the conclusion, LifeSite is thus a metaphor for the broader ineffectiveness of sanctions in changing the culture of contempt.

CHAPTER EIGHT

Case Study: "American Viganò"

There's a notoriously fine line between commentary and contempt. Commentary is a time-honored and completely legitimate literary genre, and, by definition, it's often pugnacious and hard-hitting. Some of the greatest writers in the history of the English language have engaged in commentary about events and personalities that includes withering one-liners and put-downs—think Oscar Wilde, for example, or G.K. Chesterton, or William F. Buckley Jr. We don't want such voices muzzled by a gospel of political correctness, and we don't want them pulling their punches out of an exaggerated fear of giving offense. Robust public commentary makes us think, challenges our assumptions, and acts as an antidote to lazy *a priori*. In most ways, it's unrealistic to ask commentators to be scrupulously fair—bias is baked into the cake, so to speak, because the whole point is to make a case about why a particular point of view is right and others are wrong. Being exposed to disagreeable opinion may be annoying, but it's preferable to the alternative, which is censorship, thought control, and forced homogenization of thought.

Yet as Thomas Aquinas famously laid out, every virtue has a corresponding vice, which is often a corrupt and distorted form of the virtue. Contempt could be defined as a form of commentary in which inflicting injury is more important than truth, and in which the principal aim is not to skewer ideas but the people who hold them. Distinguishing commentary from contempt is difficult, and it often comes down to an "eye of the beholder" dynamic—one person's commentary, in other words, is another's contempt. It's especially challenging when the object of alleged contempt is a public figure, and thus has no expectation of privacy; when they engage in public to-and-fro about controversial issues, thereby inviting critical reaction; and when they're clearly and voluntarily associated with one side of a deep divide, thereby making it inevitable that people on the other side won't necessarily be disposed to charity.

Such is the case, for instance, with Archbishop Charles Chaput, who retired in 2020 as the Archbishop of Philadelphia, but who remains a bête noire for the Catholic left, especially in the United States.

Chaput is a clear conservative who has publicly advocated Communion bans for pro-choice Catholic politicians, going so far in some instances as to admonish Catholics that it's "sinful" to vote for pro-choice Democrats, even if—perhaps especially if—they're also

Roman Catholics. He's outspoken in his opposition to same-sex marriage, he's criticized the use of argot such as "LGBTQ" in Church documents, and he supported the firing of a Catholic school teacher in Pennsylvania in 2015 for being openly lesbian and in a same-sex marriage. He's blamed the clerical sexual scandals in Catholicism, at least in part, on what he called in 2019 "a pattern of predatory homosexuality and a failure to weed that out from church life." He's also defended EWTN, the right-wing Catholic media empire, saying complaints that it's anti–Pope Francis are "vindictive and false." Over the years, both during his fourteen years in Denver and his nine in Philadelphia, Chaput has favored individuals and organizations perceived as conservative and turned a cold shoulder to those seen as more liberal.

In other words, if a Catholic bishop in America ever voluntarily put a rhetorical target on his own back, it's arguably Charles Chaput.

In a sense, that's precisely what makes Chaput an apt test case for the distinction between commentary and contempt. It's easy to play fair with people who stay out of the firing line and never criticize anyone or anything; it's far more difficult to do so when the very sight of someone, or the sound of their voice, makes your skin crawl. Yet virtue is a demanding master, and how we treat the lightning rods of the world is a far more realistic assessment of how much we've mastered it than how we deal with hail fellows well met.

By an indirect route, these reflections bring us to a contemptuous narrative that's grown up about Chaput in the Pope Francis era, to wit, that he's the "American Viganò." The phrase was coined by Michael Sean Winters of the left-leaning *National Catholic Reporter* in December 2020, but it was the logical culmination of a drumbeat of commentary on Chaput by liberal critics. The reference is to Italian Archbishop Carlo Maria Viganò, a former papal nuncio (ambassador) to the United States, who famously accused Pope Francis of malfeasance in the handling of sexual abuse allegations against ex-Cardinal (and ex-priest) Theodore McCarrick, calling on Francis to resign, and who's gone to become an embittered critic of the pontiff across multiple fronts, associating himself with far-right sentiment both secular and ecclesiastical on all manner of issues.

Before proceeding, I need to read two caveats into the record.

First, I have a personal relationship with Chaput that goes beyond reporter/source dynamics. I was educated by the Capuchin Franciscans on the high plains of western Kansas, about sixty miles from where Chaput himself grew up, and I've known him for decades. I'm by temperament and outlook a moderate, Chaput a strong conservative, so we sometimes haven't seen eye-to-eye, but he's always been very supportive, and I've always found him smart, curious, and honest. At one point, I was part of a small men's group that dined with Chaput once a month in the Archdiocese of Denver. If it is required to dislike someone in order to be objective about them, then I'm disqualified in Chaput's case.

Second, I also have a personal connection with Winters, since at one point he was my colleague at the *National Catholic Reporter.* Winters occasionally has been critical of both Crux and me personally, though never in anything I'd consider a contemptuous fashion. In any event, he's hardly the only example of a liberal American Catholic who's taken issue with Chaput—it's just that in typical Winters fashion, his is perhaps the most rhetorically effective critique, given his impressive command of language and his deep knowledge of Catholic affairs. I don't believe anything here is driven by personal considerations, but it would be less than honest not to acknowledge our history.

With those stipulations out of the way, let's unpack the "American Viganò" charge against Chaput and why it serves as an example of today's culture of contempt.

BACKGROUND

Charles Joseph Chaput was born in 1944 in Concordia, Kansas, a small town nestled in the northeastern part of the state about a hundred miles from my own hometown of Hays to the south and west. His father was *Quebecois*, or French Canadian, allegedly a distant descendant of King Louis IX of France, and worked in Kansas as a mortician and embalmer. His mother was a Native American, a member of the Prairie Band Potawatomi

Nation, and his maternal grandmother was the last member of the tribe to live on a reservation. Chaput was made a member of the tribe as a child, given the name "rustling wind." (Exactly how much native ancestry Chaput can claim has sometimes been questioned; his fellow Capuchins once told me they used to joke that Chaput needed to be careful not to cut himself shaving, or he'd lose all his Indian blood.)

Chaput joined the Capuchin Franciscans in 1965, the year the Second Vatican Council ended (and, coincidentally, the year I was born). He studied at St. Fidelis College Seminary in Pennsylvania, the Capuchin College in Washington, DC, and the University of San Francisco. People who knew the young Chaput say that he went through what might be called a "liberal" phase as a young man, volunteering for the presidential campaign of Robert F. Kennedy in 1968 and supporting the election of Jimmy Carter in 1976, both Democrats. He held various leadership positions in the Capuchin order during the 1970s and '80s, and he was part of a group of Native American Catholics who met the late Pope John Paul II, now St. John Paul, when the Polish pontiff visited Phoenix in 1987.

Probably because of that experience, John Paul named Chaput the bishop of Rapid City, South Dakota, where almost 10 percent of the city's population is Native American, and where nearby Bear Butte State Park remains an important place of gathering and worship for many Native American tribes. Chaput was only the second priest of Native American ancestry to be named a Catholic bishop in the United States, but one interesting feature of his ecclesiastical trajectory is that he never really traded on his ancestry—from early on, he became better known as a conservative leader than as the representative of an ethnic minority.

In 1987, John Paul named Chaput the Archbishop of Denver, replacing Archbishop James Stafford, who'd been called to Rome to become the head of the Pontifical Council for Laity and who was eventually made a cardinal. Chaput rapidly transformed Denver into a hub for the conservative energies swirling in the Catholic Church under John Paul II, providing a home for missionary organizations, media outlets, academics, and others who broadly formed part of the push for Catholic identity and the evangelization of culture. He was a figure of trust for the John Paul II papacy; among other things, he was tasked in 2007 with leading an apostolic visitation (Vatican-speak for "investigation") in the Australian diocese of Toowoomba under Bishop Bill Morris, who had suggested consideration of the ordination of women as priests. Though Morris said he never saw Chaput's final report, it apparently set the stage for Morris' removal as bishop in 2011.

Yet Chaput was always no mere ideologue. In 1997, for example, when the internet was first emerging as the revolutionary technology it would eventually become, Chaput hosted a conference in Denver on the "new technologies" featuring fifty bishops and archbishops and seven cardinals, including the illustrious Cardinal Jean-Marie Lustiger of Paris, as well as secular experts such as Esther Dyson and Neil Postman. Chaput demonstrated a capacity to defy ideological labels, at one point standing up during a panel discussion led by software moguls to challenge them about how their technological prowess might serve the poor.

In 2011, Pope Benedict XVI gave Chaput what many observers at the time regarded as perhaps the least desirable—or, to put it differently, most challenging—assignment in the Catholic Church in the US, which was taking over as the Archbishop of Philadelphia. The archdiocese had been hit with two damning Grand Jury reports in 2005 and earlier in 2011 accusing it of inaction and cover-up on multiple cases of clerical sexual abuse. In addition, the two previous archbishops, Cardinals Anthony Bevilacqua and Justin Rigali, had left behind crippling deficits that meant whoever took over would have to make some deeply unpopular choices. Chaput removed priests accused of abuse, closed forty-nine schools, and sold the archbishop's mansion for $10 million as part of a plan to reduce the operating budget deficit. By most accounts, he did what he could to stop the bleeding, though he was never made a cardinal like his two predecessors, which some took as a snub for Chaput's reputed antipathy to the Francis papacy.

In all fairness, Chaput hosted Pope Francis when the pontiff visited Philadelphia in 2015 for an edition of the Vatican-sponsored World Meeting of Families, describing the pope's presence as "historic and exhilarating," and he insisted that Francis "embodies the message of mercy, joy and love that lies at the heart of the Gospel." As a Franciscan himself, Chaput said at the time, hosting a pope named Francis was a dream come true. However, tensions were also apparent along the way. For example, in the run-up to the event, Chaput made clear that while gay and lesbian people would be welcome at the event, along with everyone else, no platform would be provided for anyone who wanted to challenge Church teaching on sexuality and marriage. Further, Francis landed in Philadelphia after issuing his apostolic exhortation *Amoris Laetitia*, which offered a cautious green light for the reception of Communion by divorced and civilly remarried Catholics under certain conditions. The document was the product of two Synods of Bishops in Rome, after which Chaput had said during a lecture in Manhattan that "confusion is of the devil" and that "the public image that came across [of the synods] was one of confusion." In the minds of Pope Francis fans, such language meant the prelate hosting the pope in Philly had just accused him of being of the devil. Later, in 2018, when Chaput was selected as a delegate to the pope's Synod of Bishops on Youth, Chaput publicly called on Francis to cancel the event, warning that bishops would have "absolutely no credibility" discussing the topic, and to host a summit

on the life of bishops instead in the wake of the McCarrick fiasco.

Like all bishops in the Catholic Church, Chaput
submitted his resignation in September 2019 when he
reached the age of seventy-five, which is the mandatory
retirement age. Unlike most prelates, however, Chaput's
resignation was accepted almost immediately—three
months later he was out, replaced by Archbishop Nelson
Perez, who had previously been the Bishop of Cleveland
and who became the first Hispanic Archbishop of Philadelphia. Under other circumstances, relieving Chaput
of the burden of office in Philly might have been seen
as an act of mercy by a grateful pope, knowing the
hardship duty the office had represented for almost a
decade and freeing Chaput up to do the things he loves
most. Instead, it was spun as a rebuke. Here's how the
New York Times characterized the move: "Pope Francis
Replaces Conservative Archbishop of Philadelphia.
Archbishop Charles J. Chaput, who was appointed by
Pope Benedict XVI in 2011, has long been known as
a theological and political conservative, often at odds
with Pope Francis." For the record, however, Chaput has
insisted that he was the one who urged Francis to name
a replacement quickly, saying, "I thought the church in
Philadelphia needed leadership for the future and I just
couldn't do that because of my age."

Among those liberal Catholic figures not shedding
any tears when Chaput stepped down was Winters.
In August 2016, he responded to a column in which

Chaput had offered reflections ahead of the November 2016 election after referencing two pro-choice Catholic Democrats: then-Vice President Joe Biden and the party's vice-presidential nominee in 2016, Tim Kaine.

Here's how Winters ended his piece.

> I admit that I find it tiresome to have to continually criticize Archbishop Chaput. I do so in sadness not in anger. But, it must be said: If I were writing a work of fiction and I wanted to create a caricature of a culture warrior bishop, I do not think I would have the courage to create one so reckless, so un-complicated in his moral sensibilities (and not in a good way), and so quick to render judgment against others, so willing to ignore the pope, or to cite him, as it suits his own purposes, so intellectually thin and so edgily partisan, as Archbishop Chaput's columns show him to be.

THE ACCUSATION

That rehearsal of Chaput's history brings us to December 2020, when Chaput penned an article for *First Things*, a conservative American Catholic publication, titled "Mr. Biden and the Matter of Scandal." The headline itself would prove controversial, since by December 2020 it seemed clear to most neutral observers that Biden had actually won the November 2020 election and therefore merited the title "president-elect." However, the burden of Chaput's article wasn't to dispute the validity of the vote, but rather to address the question of whether pro-choice Catholic politicians such as Biden should be denied Communion.

To be clear, Chaput wasn't arguing for an inflexible position: "Publicly denying Communion to public officials is not always wise or the best pastoral course," he wrote. "Doing so in a loud and forceful manner may cause more harm than good by inviting the official to bask in the media glow of victimhood." However, Chaput went on to reject, forcefully, "any seeming indifference to the issue, any hint in a national bishops' statement or policy that would give bishops permission to turn their heads away from the gravity of a very serious issue."

Chaput went on to rehearse the history of the dispute within American Catholicism since 2004, when the pro-choice Catholic John Kerry was nominated by the Democrats to challenge incumbent Republican President George Bush, and criticized the parts played in that controversy by McCarrick and also Cardinal Donald Wuerl, who took over from McCarrick in Washington, DC, until his own retirement in 2018 amid criticism of his role in managing abuse cases, including that of McCarrick.

"Public figures who identify as 'Catholic' give scandal to the faithful when receiving Communion by creating the impression that the moral laws of the

Church are optional. And bishops give similar scandal by not speaking up publicly about the issue and danger of sacrilege," Chaput wrote. "When bishops publicly announce their willingness to give Communion to Mr. Biden, without clearly teaching the gravity of his facilitating the evil of abortion (and his approval of same-sex relationships), they do a serious disservice to their brother bishops and their people. . . . Many of his actions and words have also supported or smoothed the way for grave moral evils in our public life that have resulted in the destruction of millions of innocent lives. Mr. Biden has said that he will continue to advance those same policies as president, and thus should not receive Holy Communion. His stated intention requires a strong and consistent response from Church leaders and faithful."

"Reception of Communion is not a right but a gift and privilege; and on the subject of 'rights,' the believing community has a priority right to the integrity of its belief and practice," Chaput concluded.

The *First Things* essay brought a bristling response from Winters on December 9, 2020. Much of the language is obviously intended to lampoon Chaput's position, which Winters describes as "presumptuous," an example of "cultural blindness," and "ludicrous." Toward the end, Winters accuses Chaput of "bad theology," "misunderstanding of American politics," "weaponization of pastoral issues," and the sour grapes of a "prelate who did not rise to the ranks his friends thought his due." (Winters makes the point that while Wuerl became a cardinal, Chaput never did, and suggests that Chaput may have been trying to "slime" Wuerl by associating him with McCarrick.)

While some pious souls might object that one should not use such rhetoric in describing a successor of the Apostles, the truth is that Chaput brought it on himself. He entered the fray not as a bishop but as a commentator on Catholic affairs, which means he's obliged to suffer the slings and arrows of outrageous fortune along with the rest of us. Whether Winters' piece would have been stronger without some of the overcharged vocabulary is a question for his copyeditor, not his priest or moral theologian.

However, there was a point where controversy crossed into contempt, and it came both in the headline of Winters' piece and also the penultimate line: "Chaput has become an American Viganò, and, like the disgraced former nuncio, he is dividing the episcopacy even in retirement."

In some ways, it was probably inevitable that critics of Chaput would link him with Viganò, since guilt by association is a time-honored rhetorical trope. If you disagree with a political conservative, you call him or her a Nazi; if it's a liberal, she or he is a Commie. It's tempting to shrug off such verbiage under the principle of "Goodwin's Law," a web term that, loosely, implies that the first person to make a comparison to the Nazis in an internet discussion loses that argument. However,

Winters' reference was not a one-off casual aside, but rather the climax of a long accumulation of suggestions from Chaput critics persistently trying to link him to Viganò and his agenda.

In July 2019, Villanova historian and frequent liberal Catholic commentator Massimo Faggioli penned an essay for *La Croix* in which he named three American bishops as having "sided" with Viganò's call for Pope Francis to resign in August 2018, including Chaput on that list in addition to Archbishop Salvatore Cordileone of San Francisco and Bishop Joseph Strickland of Tyler, Texas. Faggioli termed the three prelates "devout schismatics . . . [who] openly promote the undermining of the bishop of Rome among the Catholic faithful." That piece brought strong objections from Chaput and his supporters, who insisted that Chaput was not part of the Viganò agenda. In response, Mike Lewis of the blog *Where Peter Is* posted an essay titled "The Archbishop Doth Protest Too Much," suggesting that tying Chaput to Viganò might not be entirely unwarranted and that Chaput's "public record has shown some very clear signs of resistance to—and even subversion of—Pope Francis and his teachings."

Two months later, during a panel discussion at the University of Notre Dame on the clerical sexual abuse crisis, Chilean survivor Juan Carlos Cruz, a close adviser to Pope Francis, publicly accused certain "conservative bishops," specifically mentioning Italian Archbishop Carlo Maria Viganò, American Cardinal Raymond

Burke, and Archbishop Charles Chaput of Philadelphia, of "weaponizing" the suffering of abuse victims for purposes of delivering ideological attacks on the pontiff. Once again, the suggestion was that Chaput and Viganò breathe the same political air and that their outlooks on Pope Francis are similar.

Thus, by the time Winters labeled Chaput the "American Viganò," the ground had been laid for that claim to find a receptive audience among progressive-minded Catholics and Pope Francis admirers, most of whom probably aren't inclined to make careful distinctions among figures perceived as papal critics (or, at least, as having reservations about the papacy.) Further, the label stuck. When the Associated Press covered the transition from Chaput to Perez in Philadelphia, its article asserted that Chaput had "praised the integrity of leading Francis critic Archbishop Carlo Maria Viganò," thus once again linking the two prelates in the public eye. Though it's too early to be sure, it's not out of the question that when Chaput dies, the lead paragraph of his obituary may well once again put him in Viganò's company.

FROM COMMENTARY TO CONTEMPT

Here's why tying Chaput to Viganò is not merely scurrilous but contemptuous.

To begin with, when Viganò first issued his *J'accuse* against Pope Francis in 2018, it was in the context of the clerical sexual abuse scandals. The charge was that Viganò had informed the pope of rumors of misconduct about McCarrick in 2013, yet Francis did not take any action until those charges became public five years later. On the basis of that claim, Viganò called on Pope Francis to resign. In assessing how Chaput responded, it's important to remember that when he arrived in Philadelphia, he inherited an archdiocese reeling from years of abuse scandals, and the battle for reform was a large part of Chaput's agenda.

"As a bishop, the only honest way I can talk about the abuse tragedy is to start by apologizing for the failure of the Church and her leaders—apologizing to victims, and apologizing to the Catholic community," Chaput said when he took over the reins.

Like many American bishops at the time, Chaput's initial response to the Viganò accusation was cautious, since the last thing a leader attempting to reach out to victims would want is to be perceived as dismissing an abuse charge out of hand or failing to take it seriously. Yet even by that standard, what Chaput said publicly about Viganò in the summer of 2018 was muted. A spokesman for the Archdiocese of Philadelphia said only that Chaput "enjoyed working with Archbishop Viganò during his tenure as Apostolic Nuncio," which was 2011–2016, adding that Chaput found Viganò's tenure "to be marked by integrity to the Church." As to the specific charge, Chaput said he could not comment "on

Archbishop Viganò's recent testimonial as it is beyond his personal experience."

To call that "siding" with Viganò clearly is an exaggeration. Instead, the most reasonable explanation is that Chaput wanted to demonstrate sensitivity to an abuse allegation without associating himself with the broader agenda with which it came wrapped in Viganò's original manifesto. Chaput never echoed the call for Francis to resign, never suggested the pope was complicit in an abuse cover-up, and has not commented on Viganò at all since that initial reaction in August 2018, despite the fact that Viganò has kept up a steady drumbeat of commentary on affairs both ecclesiastical and political ever since.

If Chaput is a Viganò ally, in other words, he's an unusually silent partner, which is all the more odd given that Chaput is not normally shy about saying what he thinks.

Second, since that original charge against the pope in 2018, Viganò has gone on to become a leading voice of the Catholic hard-right on multiple fronts. Among other things, he's emerged as a deep admirer of former President Donald Trump, writing a lengthy letter of praise during the 2020 presidential campaign that Trump retweeted to his supporters. Chaput, by way of contrast, has never been a Trump enthusiast, once referring to him as "an eccentric businessman of defective ethics whose bombast and buffoonery make him inconceivable as president." While Chaput clearly is no fan of most Democratic opposition to Trump either, it's only the zero-sum logic of secular politics that says that if he criticizes a pro-choice Catholic Democrat, he therefore must be endorsing Trump and his allies.

Third, Chaput also clashed publicly with Trump on a core element of the former president's domestic agenda: immigration. Chaput is basically pro-immigrant, and in the run-up to the 2016 election he called Trump's proposal to cancel automatic citizenship for the children of immigrants born in the United States a "profoundly bad idea." In June 2018, he published a column on the Trump administration's policy of separating immigrant families during deportation procedures. "There's a human cost to political theater that can be inexcusably ugly, especially when it's paid by children," Chaput wrote at the time. "The administration's most recent blunder—separating children from their parents caught illegally entering the country—was both stupid and de-structive, and the storm of anger it sparked, warranted." In 2020, Chaput insisted that regularizing the status of most undocumented immigrants in America is a "moral imperative."

For the record, this is also another area of contrast with Viganò, who is also strongly anti-immigrant. In 2021, for example, Viganò tweeted that "illegal immigration as well—which is supported in order to destabilize nations & cancel their identities—finds support from both the Left as well as the Church of

Bergoglio, despite the fact that it is directly connected with the trafficking of minors."

Chaput has also broken with Trump and the Republican Party over a number of other issues, including the death penalty. In 2019 he wrote, "What the death penalty does achieve is closure through bloodletting, and violence against violence—which is not really closure at all, because murder will continue as long as humans sin, and capital punishment can never, by its nature, strike at murder's root. Only love can do that." He's also supported greater gun control, writing, "I buried some of the young Columbine victims twenty years ago. I sat with their families, watched them weep, listened to their anger, and saw the human wreckage that gun violence leaves behind. The experience taught me that assault rifles are not a birthright, and the Second Amendment is not a Golden Calf. I support thorough background checks and more restrictive access to guns for anyone seeking to purchase them." (He also added that gun control by itself won't solve the problem of violence, because we also have to address the "moral agents with twisted hearts" who use those weapons.)

In a 2021 interview, Chaput summed up his political journey, having started as a stalwart Democrat and ending up alienated to a certain extent from both political parties. "As I got older, I began to see that there was no integrity in the Democrat party in terms of the values that were really important to me, and oftentimes not in the Republican party either," he said.

There certainly have been moments when Chaput took positions seen as pro-Trump, including suggesting that criticism of Supreme Court nominee Amy Coney Barrett was "anti-Catholic" and also defending former Attorney General William Barr's invitation in September 2020 to speak at the National Catholic Prayer Breakfast. That's to be expected from a public figure who's essentially a political conservative, but to suggest that Chaput somehow has the same outlook on the Trump phenomenon as Viganò is obviously false.

Fourth, Viganò is a favorite of hard-right and traditionalist Catholic news outlets such as LifeSite and Church Militant, as well as think tanks and advocacy groups such as the Lepanto Institute, while Chaput is among their most determined critics. Here's what Chaput wrote of such groups in 2015 in the run-up to the World Meeting of Families in Philadelphia, after Church Militant charged that the event was "infested" with pro-abortion and pro-gay figures: "The sole desire of both Lepanto and Church Militant is to create division, confusion, and conflict within the Church. Actions of that nature run contrary to Christian tradition. Their reports are not to be taken seriously," Chaput said.

"Both Lepanto and Church Militant sow division wherever they tread. They do not seem to acknowledge the need to work with civic society and its representatives on a project like the World Meeting of Families. And we are not going to spend/waste time arguing with them. They are sincere, but also destructive," he said. For his trouble, in 2021 Church Militant founder Michael Voris accused Chaput of being part of the "Catholic establishment" seeking to cover up the truth about "combating evil in the hierarchy."

Fifth, Viganò is also known for skepticism about the science behind the coronavirus pandemic and for fears of a looming one-world government seeking to exploit the crisis to impose a global totalitarian regime. Chaput has never voiced any such sentiments. He was among those Catholic bishops in the US who voiced concern about the restrictions on religious freedom imposed as part of the early response to the pandemic, suggesting that some American bishops had been "too compliant." But he also said it's essential for Christians to be "cooperative" with public authorities during a health crisis in order to serve the common good, and he also voiced support for mask mandates, calling them "necessary to a certain point."

Sixth, Viganò is an acerbic critic of the Second Vatican Council (1962–1965), saying in 2020 that "hostile forces" at the council caused "the abdication of the Catholic Church" through a "sensational deception." Moreover, he said, "The errors of the post-conciliar period were contained *in nuce* in the Conciliar Acts," suggesting the problem wasn't simply the implementation of the council but its own teaching. By way of contrast, here's what Chaput said of Vatican II in a 2021 interview with Pablo Kay of Angelus, the news platform of the Archdiocese of Los Angeles: "I think the Second Vatican Council is the most precious gift that the Holy Spirit has given the Church in my lifetime. I was ordained a priest in 1970, so the last part of my seminary formation was very much influenced by the council, and I'm grateful that I was exposed to all the documents of the council while I was still in school."

Here's the bottom line: Chaput is an outspoken figure who invites strong reactions—as he said in 2021, comparing himself to fellow Catholic bishops, "I talk more than the others do." Criticism of his views is entirely fair, and indeed, healthy. If the abuse scandals have taught us anything, it's the toxic consequences of an exaggerated deference to clerical opinion. However, like anyone else, Chaput should be held responsible for his own statements and expressions, not anyone else's agenda. To imply that he embraces the outlook of a figure with whom he so obviously, and so frequently, disagrees is a classic example of the culture of contempt in action.

Conclusion

As we've seen through the course of this informal traipse across the Catholic media landscape, a wider culture of contempt shapes, and distorts, Catholic coverage in multiple ways. It can generate ugly and misleading narratives about public figures, up to and definitely including popes, but also other targets, such as the editor of a leading Italian Catholic newspaper. It can spawn aggressive platforms whose mission, seemingly, is to excoriate perceived enemies and keep users in a state of perpetual outrage. It can even affect the news judgment and editorial decision-making of more mainstream platforms that, typically, uphold the basic principles of ethical journalistic practice. In social media spaces, it induces people to say almost unimaginably hurtful and cruel things about one another—often, by the way, without knowing if those hurtful and cruel things are even true.

One other potentially toxic consequence of the culture of contempt, which we haven't quite yet explored, is the way in which it can induce news organizations to pull their punches, to avoid taking risks out of fear of backlash, which, among other things, might threaten their funding and livelihoods. Let me take an example from personal experience.

As I've mentioned, my own news site, Crux, was born as a special project of the *Boston Globe* in 2014. Alas, we apparently lost the favor of the gods of journalism somewhere along the way, because in 2016, as the *Globe* was passing through a financial crunch, we were informed that Crux was being discontinued and the staff was being laid off. Softening the blow somewhat was the incredibly gracious manner in which the *Globe* handled the situation, including offering to give me the rights to the Crux brand and site essentially for free. They even offered to continue hosting and servicing the site until we could migrate it to our own set of servers. The difficulty was that we only had a little over two weeks to find alternate sources of funding, or we would be out of business.

By that stage our luck seemed to return: within a matter of days, we had sponsorship deals with the Knights of Columbus and the DeSales Media Group at the Diocese of Brooklyn, along with lesser levels of support from the Archdioceses of Los Angeles, New York, and Washington, DC. We incorporated in the state of Colorado, and we were back in business. I sometimes joke that we actually experienced a corporate resurrection, in that we died and rose again on the third business day.

I came into the experience of taking over at Crux with a vague sense of what I wanted it to be, shaped

largely by the principles outlined in the Mission Statement in chapter one. I was also conscious that we faced
a hermeneutic of suspicion in some quarters related to
where we were getting our money, in that it was tough
for some people, especially more liberal Catholics, to
believe that the Knights of Columbus, generally known
for supporting fairly conservative news outlets, wouldn't
try to push our editorial policies in that direction. I also
knew that no matter how hard we tried, some conservatives would be suspicious of Crux both because of my
own background at the *National Catholic Reporter* and
because of our history with the *Boston Globe*, which,
over the years, hasn't exactly been perceived as a great
friend of the Catholic Church.

Realizing all that, I felt it was important that we do
three things right away in an effort to "rebrand" Crux:

- Build a towering wall of separation between
  news and editorial content, with the news being
  presented in as nonpartisan a fashion as possible,
  while still leaving scope for authorial personality.
  After all, if we were simply going to photocopy
  the sort of coverage one can already find in wire
  services and other outlets, what was the point?

- Carry no staff editorials, so that no piece of opinion would ever be published in the name of Crux.
  To the extent possible, I wanted our "agenda" to
  be completely apolitical and not identified with
  any camp or current within the Church.

- In our opinion content, seek and publish the contributions of the strongest voices on all sides of an argument, so that people would come to see Crux as a space in which everyone gets an equal shot.

Toward that last aim, we solicited pieces from the likes of Jesuit Fr. James Martin and Pope Francis biographer and enthusiast Austen Ivereigh on the Catholic left, and outspoken Catholic conservatives such as Fr. Dwight Longenecker and Tom Williams. We worked awfully hard to maintain a sense of fair play, constantly asking ourselves, for example, after a strongly liberal piece had appeared, whom among our conservative roster we could hit up to balance the scales. In retrospect, however, I now see that strategy was always doomed to failure because it would never be acceptable to the culture of contempt.

Although we got low-level complaints about this or that piece from the beginning, the storm really broke in 2016 and early 2017 with the publication of Pope Francis' apostolic exhortation *Amoris Laetitia*. It capped two raucous, highly acrimonious Synods of Bishops on the family in 2014 and 2015, which, among other things, featured charges from conservatives that the synods were "rigged" to support the predetermined outcomes the pope wanted. In the end, Pope Francis in *Amoris* opened a cautious door to the reception of Communion by Catholics who divorce and remarry outside the Church and who remain in that new marriage. He did so over the fervent objections of many conservatives that such a step not only betrayed Church teaching on marriage—which, based on the words of Christ in the Gospel, is "What God has joined together, let no one separate"—but also was at odds with an explicit earlier ruling by Pope John Paul II on the same question.

As this debate was unfolding, Crux published almost daily contributions from the protagonists. Admittedly, some of this content was strong medicine: at one point Longenecker called the confusion created in the wake of the document a "shipwreck" and suggested Francis and his allies were attempting to introduce "change by stealth," while Ivereigh, for his part, accused critics of *Amoris* of being locked into "death-trap" logic and, at another point, noting that many of those critics are converts, suggested they were suffering from "convert neurosis." Obviously, I knew such rhetoric would ruffle feathers, but it was undeniably the sort of thing being said at the time, whether we published it or not, and the aim was to demonstrate fairness by allowing it free rein on both sides.

What happened was, looking back, entirely predictable. Some liberals concluded we had joined the conservative opposition to Francis; at one point I actually got an angry phone call from a Vatican official very close to the pope who wanted to point out that, by his count at that stage, we had published six or seven articles critical of *Amoris* and only four or five that were supportive. (In reality, of the pieces he was counting as "critical," two were largely factual breakdowns of the document that contained no judgments one way or the other. In the middle of a war, however, I suppose even neutrality can look like taking sides.) On the other side, conservatives turned Ivereigh into a bête noire. It didn't help that, at the time, Ivereigh was still listed as an associate editor of Crux, a role he'd played at the beginning of Crux as an independent operation; by the time *Amoris* rolled around, he was almost entirely consumed by his biographies of Francis and his growing role as a preeminent English-language commentator on the papacy. Nevertheless, those titles led many conservatives to believe that whatever Ivereigh said, including on his hyperactive Twitter account, somehow represented the corporate editorial line of Crux.

At this stage, John Zuhlsdorf of *Fr. Z's Blog* took up the argument, insisting it was outrageous that a news platform funded by the Knights of Columbus would publish someone such as Ivereigh. He called upon his readers—and they are many—to flood the Knights with angry phone calls, emails, and letters demanding that Crux be defunded. To the great credit of the Knights, who, at the time, were represented in their dealings with Crux by the late Andrew Walther, who was a good personal friend, they never directly tried to sway our editorial decisions. However, it was abundantly clear that Crux was becoming a bigger headache for them than they really had any stomach for, and, not long afterward, they told us they were relocating their funding for us to support for Christians in the Middle East. It would be dishonest not to say that losing our chief benefactor represented an existential threat, and it triggered an immediate reexamination of our editorial policies.

The chief consequence was that beginning immediately, Crux discontinued publishing all guest opinion pieces. (I fancy that my own contributions to the site are analysis, not opinion, in that I never draw conclusions about who's right or wrong in a given argument, but they do stray beyond strict reporting.) From that moment to this day, we have never since published a piece in which the author takes a position on a disputed point, and we really don't publish guest pieces of any sort to avoid the risk of guilt by association. I want to be clear that I'm not presenting this decision as some sort of noble journalistic gesture. On the contrary, I regard it as Crux's greatest failure to date that we haven't figured out a way to create a "Catholic commons" in which all the voices in a conversation can interact with one another in a spirit of respect.

Admittedly, I'm precisely the wrong guy to be able to be objective about this, but it seemed that underlying the anti-Crux campaign was a core principle of the culture of contempt: people with whom you disagree aren't just wrong; they're evil—and they must be stopped. On this view, one responds to such people not with argument but with the media equivalent of brute force, including attempting to shut them down. In such an environment, it would be naïve to believe that the threat of such violence doesn't have an effect in terms of making news judgments—either to avoid such fallout, or to deliberately incite it against someone else in order to bolster one's own bottom line.

WHAT WON'T WORK

It would be great if there were a magic-bullet solution to the culture of contempt, at least insofar as it infects the Catholic media world. Unfortunately, after having thought about this problem off and on for the better part of twenty years, and after having experienced myself in a couple different ways its hard edge, I find myself far clearer about what not to do than what might actually work.

To begin, I think it's abundantly obvious that calling out news platforms that subsist on the culture of contempt, publicly saying they're mean or even "un-Catholic," has no discernible effect other than to make the situation worse. Writing in 2016, Fr. Dwight Longenecker said this: "The venomous and vitriolic bloggers will most assuredly not accept criticism, but [they will] lash back with a fuller fury and loftier righteousness. Impervious to both gentle reproof and harsh attack, they will, like cornered animals, snarl, and bite back." It's not often that one finds such oracular truth in a snappy eight-hundred-word newspaper column, but there it is.

There are two caveats I'll offer to the general ineffectiveness of this sort of "fraternal correction." The first is that it may not reach platforms wholly beholden to the culture of contempt, but for those still attempting to resist it, it can have positive results. At Crux, we occasionally receive reactions from readers objecting that a particular headline was overly sensationalistic, or that a particular bit of verbiage was insulting, or that leaving a certain voice out of a story reflected bias. We take that sort of input seriously, and I know well that so many of our colleagues do so as well. The problem, however, is that it's basically a case of preaching to the choir. When dealing with people who are trying to be responsible, you can sometimes help them see how they failed in a particular case. The real issue, however, is reaching people for whom responsibility does not really seem to be a high priority.

The other caveat has to do with correcting factual inaccuracy. Arguing with people about their tone and approach may be generally a waste of time, but responding to inaccurate information put into circulation by one platform or another is not. Whether it be what Pope John Paul II said (or didn't say) about a Mel Gibson movie, what Pope Francis said (or didn't say) about pets going to heaven, the reality of Pope Benedict XVI's alleged affiliation with the Nazi Party, how much money the Vatican actually has (as best we can determine), or whatever else, it is the obligation of news organizations to correct the record when it's distorted. That's not about convincing anyone to change their ways, which is an entirely different exercise, but rather about making sure misinformation is treated before it metastasizes and becomes conventional wisdom. In the course of doing so, however, it's important not to point fingers or speculate about someone's motives for publicizing the false or misleading claim, because it can very easily be seen as arrogant—trust me on this one, because humility isn't exactly one of my native virtues—or as rejoicing in someone else's embarrassment. On those occasions when I need to call out a false narrative, I never even identify the platform where it originated, preferring to say simply "it was reported this week" or something like that, unless it's absolutely essential to telling the story.

On a different front, ecclesiastical sanctions of news platforms are almost always ineffective and, in a great many cases, actually counterproductive. This truth, by the way, isn't limited to media organizations. I've known Catholic theologians over the years, for instance, who joke that they lie awake at night and dream of being censured by the Vatican, because it would drive their book sales through the roof. That's no joke; consider Sri Lankan theologian Fr. Tissa Balasuriya, whose book *Mary and Human Liberation*—in which, among other things, Balasuriya suggested Mary was the first female priest—had originally been printed by his own small theological center and sold just a few hundred copies. Yet when the Vatican's Congregation for the Doctrine of the Faith, headed by then–Cardinal Joseph Ratzinger, excommunicated Balasuriya in January 1997, the book was picked up by major publishers and sold in the thousands. It was widely reviewed, including by the all-important *Publisher's Weekly*, and to this day is available on Amazon and other online retailers. Getting slapped down by the powers that be, from a strictly commercial point of view, is often the gift that keeps on giving.

As we've already noted, in the logic of the culture of contempt, if you're convinced that ecclesiastic official-dom is a core part of the problem—if, like some conservatives, you regard the bishops as hopelessly infected by liberalism and secularism and generally feckless in the face of heresy, or if, like many liberals, you regard the bishops as benighted conservatives unwilling, or unable, to embrace urgently needed reforms in Church teaching and practice—then how are you going to react when a bishop, or group of bishops, tells you something is bad? In most cases, you'll instinctively regard it as likely to be good, and you'll be far more interested in it than you would have been left to your own devices.

Much the same could be said of sanctions from social media platforms and hosting services. As we saw in the case study on LifeSite News, suspensions and bans from platforms such as Twitter and Facebook are generally ineffective in reducing visibility and appeal, to say nothing of changing behavior. Not only are there now alternative platforms for voices excluded from the more mainstream services, but fans of the culture of contempt will simply be contemptuous of anyone who tries to muscle them out of the conversation, and they will cheer on media outlets that resist this sort of attempted muzzling too.

One might think that journalists should do a better job of policing themselves, the same way that, say, lawyers do through the bar association, or that doctors do through medical associations. In those cases, complaints against a particular attorney or law firm can be brought to a board composed of other attorneys who will review the evidence, deliberate, and, if necessary, mete out sanctions. There are three reasons, however, why this won't fly either. First, unlike lawyers and doctors, there's no requirement to hold a professional license to practice as a journalist, so there's really nothing meaningful to take away. At best, a reporter who violated some serious professional standard might be shunned by colleagues and find it difficult to get a new job, but if whatever happened is actually consistent with the editorial standards of the outlet the journalist works for, then there's not much else the press corps can do about it.

Second, journalists aren't supposed to make news; we're supposed to report it. If a sanction needs to be imposed on a journalist, then it ought to be done either by their own news outlet or by the institution they cover. Moreover, one of the glories of journalism is that it's generally an extremely collegial profession in which we help one another because, while today it might be you who needs the phone number of a source or copies of documents relevant to a story, tomorrow it might be me. Anything that distorts this collegial relationship is generally to be avoided. For example, in the Vatican press corps we recently had a dust-up over whether our small journalists' association ought to impose some sort of sanction on anyone who violates the embargo on a papal trip. (Since Pope Francis holds news conferences aboard the papal plane on his way back from an overseas trip, we generally agree among ourselves on a short embargo on whatever he says of an hour or two after we land, to give people time to get their bags and get to their homes or offices in order to have their packages ready to go.) There were good arguments on both sides, but I came down against the idea of journalists imposing sanctions on one another. If a reporter violates a Vatican-imposed embargo, then it's up to the Vatican if it wishes to do something about it; otherwise, I felt, we really shouldn't be in the position of policing one another, except through the informal means of not sharing information with that reporter again.

Third, journalists, of all people, are supposed to believe in freedom of the press, and it's just unnatural for one journalist to be punishing another for publishing or broadcasting (or, in this day and age, tweeting) something. Again, freedom of the press is not absolute, and if a reporter or columnist or news outlet abuses that freedom by publishing false, damaging, or dangerous content, there are legal remedies one can pursue. That, however, is a matter for the courts, not for us.

What about financial pressure? News platforms have to pay the bills, after all, and so it's natural to wonder if there's a way to punish contemptuous content by turning off the financial spigot—sort of like the Western world is attempting to do, as of this writing, through massive economic sanctions imposed on Russia following its invasion of Ukraine. As I described above, the threat of financial loss certainly influenced Crux's decision not to carry opinion content, just as, in the past, advertiser boycotts directed at news organizations sometimes have forced them to reconsider carrying a particular personality or pursuing a particular story. When radio talk show host Don Imus made racially disparaging remarks about Rutgers' women's basketball team in 2007, advertisers began to pull out of his program en masse. CBS and MSNBC both suspended Imus and then canceled his show, demonstrating the power that such financial pressures sometimes can wield.

In all honesty, however, they probably won't do much to change things in the Catholic media world, because it's just not how business models in niche media in the twenty-first century work. Most specialized Catholic platforms do sell ads, and they can be an important revenue stream, but in virtually every case, that income is supplementary. Baseline funding comes from donors, either wealthy individuals or organizations. As long as those individuals and organizations remain pleased with the product, advertiser boycotts won't put much of a dent in the bottom line. As for user contributions, if readers or viewers want contempt for their perceived enemies, they'll keep giving no matter how much other people complain.

The bottom line is that, unlike some other societies, journalism in America is a for-profit enterprise. There's no BBC, no RAI, in the United States, no dominant journalistic outlet that sets the tone for the rest and that is dependent on public funding and thus subject to public review. Media platforms in America have to respond to what the market wants—and if at least some segment of the market wants contempt, there will always be media organizations who will deliver it.

WHAT MIGHT WORK?

Fair warning: I have no magic solution to offer, nothing that I think stands even a remote chance of dramatically altering the landscape overnight. At best, these are a few fleeting thoughts rooted in a combination of generalizing from my own personal experience and a potentially naïve sense of optimism, which really isn't a promising combination for rigorous analysis.

Be Less Contemptuous Ourselves

Let me just say at the outset that if you're inclined to take spiritual advice from a journalist, you've got even deeper problems than the culture of contempt. For the record, I'm nobody's idea of a role model of holiness,

I'm about as tone-deaf in terms of transcendence as they come, and I've got no business giving anyone else advice about living out Christian morality. Still, even I can see that before we start crusading against the broader culture on some perceived shortcoming, we should do whatever we can to scrub that force out of our own hearts and minds.

How? Well, to begin with—and not to go all traditionalist about it—perhaps it's time to revive the ancient spiritual counsel of "custody of the tongue." The phrase is sometimes used in reference to monastic silence, but when St. Benedict extolled custody of the tongue as a virtue, he also meant how we care for the other, for ourselves, and for the community when we do speak. Mostly, it's a counsel for giving oneself time before speaking, to think about the consequences before rushing to social media to post the first (often angry) thought that comes into one's mind. No great cultural force ever arises spontaneously like a tornado. It's the product of countless individual choices, creating a trajectory that then, in turn, shapes more individual choices. To change the culture, therefore, each of us needs to make different choices, attentive to the way giving free rein to contempt creates a polluted environment for everyone.

Speaking of social media, if I were somehow made King of the World for a day—a terrifying idea, by the way, and I take comfort in the fact that no such position exists, so it never can be occupied by the likes of me—my lone edict would be that everyone has to take a month-long break from social media once a year so their psyches and their souls can detox. In the end, none of us can control what others tweet, post, or blog about, or how contemptuous their content may be, but we can make two other critical decisions: Do I respond in the same vein? Do I post such material myself?

If more people could answer those questions in the negative, then the culture of contempt might begin to unravel.

Light a Candle

As the oft-cited Chinese proverb goes, "It's better to light a candle than to curse the darkness." In general, when faced with a choice between attempting to tear something down or to build something up, experience tells me the latter is almost always more satisfying in the long run, even if it's far harder, more expensive, and requires greater personal commitment.

What we really need are competitors to the purveyors of contempt on both the left and right, which can raise the questions and give voice to the concerns of the same groups of people, but without venom, character assassination, and manufactured "news." We need a thousand flowers to bloom, including individual blogs, start-up video and radio platforms, creative websites, compelling books and magazine pieces, and much more beyond.

One strategy for confronting the culture of contempt, therefore, is to focus energy on encouraging alternatives. When you see a journalist who appears to be trying to treat people with respect, who avoids loaded language, and who exercises restraint with personally compromising information, find ways to support that person. At a minimum, you can send a quick note thanking her or him. I can tell you from personal experience, it's far more common at news agencies to get complaints rather than kudos, so when they do come along, they mean a lot.

In addition, Catholics with means and who are concerned about trajectories in the media today need to provide financial support for platforms and individuals who are trying to swim against the tide. Notoriously, the problem with moderates is that they're moderate about everything, including their willingness to put their money where their mouth is, while people closer to either end of the spectrum tend to be far more passionate and thus inclined to support outlets congenial to their points of view. We may not be able to make contempt disappear—since Adam and Eve, we haven't done an especially impressive job of eradicating other forms of sin either. But we can at least ensure that a wide variety of alternatives are available, trusting that while journalism as a blood sport may be just the temper of the times, the desire for truth is eternal, and there'll always be a market for it.

On a related note, we have to do a much better job of convincing the next generation of Catholic journalists, bloggers, and social media users that it's possible to be "punchy," "edgy," and "scrappy" without being acrimonious, and without inflating news beyond its natural proportions. I believe that the Catholic Church is the most fascinating beat in journalism precisely because of its complexity. No matter what the topic, there's always a welter of competing voices, and most of them actually have good points to make. Popes, for instance, have to consider the impact of their decisions not simply in terms of how people in the US or Europe will react, but the whole world. In fact, there's probably no gig on earth other than Secretary General of the UN more complicated in that regard. Answers to disputed questions are rarely simple or clear-cut, and therein lies the drama. That's the story we need to tell—not how the other side of a given issue is composed largely of idiots, charlatans, sinners, and the hopelessly naïve. It's the difference between journalism and propaganda, and, while propaganda usually pays better, journalism is a whole lot more fun.

Better Communications

Although Church leaders may not be able to do much in terms of sanctioning contemptuous content, they certainly can help encourage responsible journalism in a much more compelling fashion than they do at present—mostly by getting their act together when it comes to communications.

Right now, consider the situations of two hypo-thetical reporters covering the Vatican. One works for a hard-right news outlet that simply wants a steady supply of verbiage about how corrupt, socialist, and dictatorial the Francis papacy is, while the other writes for a responsible platform interested in what's really going on and why. The former simply has to get out of bed in the morning and apply the standard spin to whatever the day's news turns out to be, but the latter likely will spend fruitless hours trying to get Vatican officials to open up and, in the end, will be stampeded by the competition.

What Church officials need to understand is that whatever the story may be, it's going to be told by someone. The era in which bishops could control the narrative by intimidating or ignoring the media is long over. The only choice is between cooperating with reporters who are obviously trying to get the story right or allowing others to control the narrative in ways that generally turn out to be far more damaging to the Church's interests than whatever the truth of the situation actually is.

Memo to bishops, Vatican officials, and other Catholic potentates: take reporters' phone calls, answer their emails and texts, and tell your people to do the same. Make sure your communications officer is a serious professional with regular access to you and the independence to make decisions in real time without having to wade through layers of bureaucracy. The more open and transparent you are, the less capacity others will have to distort or misrepresent. In other words, you may have little power to punish contempt, but you have a vast capacity to reward responsibility.

Tuning Them Out

There's a classic Halloween episode of *The Simpsons* in which large advertising icons come to life and start rampaging through Springfield. In a desperate bid to save the city, Bart and Lisa visit an advertising agency to get advice on how to stop the monsters, and the ad man replies, "Well sir, advertising is a funny thing. . . . If people stop paying attention to it, pretty soon it goes away." (He goes on to recommend that they get Paul Anka to record a snappy jingle with the refrain "Just don't look!"—and the monsters do indeed disappear.) You'll never find a better metaphor for the media environment of the twenty-first century.

The hard truth about the media business is this: Every culture gets the journalism it wants and, therefore, that it deserves. The culture of contempt is widespread in the media today, including the Catholic media, precisely because people consume it. That includes not just the devotees of contempt but also its most dedicated critics—who, let's face it, are often fairly contemptuous of contempt. Probably nobody retweets hard-right coverage more than outraged liberals, who often jostle with one another to see who can be the most condescending about it, while conservatives typically pounce on every liberal low blow as still more evidence of how the other side isn't just wrong but evil.

My advice? Just don't look. Stop reading or watching content that's simply going to make you angry. Perpetual anger is no way to go through life, and anyway, it only encourages the manufacturers of such content. I guarantee you: nothing frustrates someone trying to provoke a reaction more than when that reaction doesn't come. There's always the lure of the idea that "someone has to say something." But the thing is, they really don't. You're not going to change any minds, and, in the meantime, you're extending the life cycle of contempt. If mainstream media outlets would just stop their every-few-weeks cycles of "exposés" about the influence of hard-right media, for example, all of which generally recycle the same platforms with the same worried commentary of alleged experts, the visibility of those outlets probably would be cut in half overnight. Similarly, if conservative media outlets would stop relentlessly regurgitating the errors and excesses of liberal platforms, those platforms, too, would probably find steep drops in traffic and relevance.

"Just Don't Look" may feel passive and feckless, like you're actually part of the problem by choosing to ignore it. After all, ignoring Vladimir Putin's war in Ukraine was hardly a sound strategy for making it stop. But in reality, tuning out is probably the simplest and most effective tool ordinary people have at their disposal to register disapproval of the media culture of contempt—and, in the meantime, it's also a sound public health strategy to keep blood pressures down, avoid heart problems, and promote personal well-being. Your doctors will thank you, and, in the long run, the media business will thank you.

FINAL THOUGHT

As I stated at the outset, there's no easy remedy to the culture of contempt as it registers in the Catholic media world. Yet resisting it, and doing everything we can to promote better options, is a labor eminently worth undertaking. What's at stake here is our credibility not just as journalists but as Catholics, and the point applies not just to those of us in the media but to everybody.

One of the glories of the Catholic Church has always been its riotous complexity. What makes us a Church and not a sect is that we embrace the most deeply traditional theologians and the most avant-garde liberal reformers at the same time, from the Raymond Burkes of the world to the Hans Küngs, and much more beyond. Catholic means universal, and the reality of the Church demonstrates that this is not mere rhetoric. What does it say about us, then, that in the twenty-first century, large numbers of Catholics appear to reject that diversity on principle—to think that a Church without liberals and what they represent would somehow be stronger, or that a Church in which conservatives were expelled or muzzled would be richer?

What it says is that we've somehow lost the Catholic instinct. That instinct can be glimpsed from where I write here in Italy every Sunday at lunch, what the Italians call the *pranzo di domenica*, when the whole family gathers around the table to share a meal, ranging from the crusty uncle who thinks every immigrant ought to be run out of Italy on a rail to the younger brother who's an ardent communist and thinks the US is the world's great menace. Over several courses of food and some wine, they sometimes get white with rage, but there's still something in the DNA that says family is more fundamental than politics, and they manage to hold it all together. Maybe that's what's actually missing: the sense that this isn't a political party or lobbying outfit we're talking about but a family, spiritual but nonetheless very real. In other words, the culture of contempt, insofar as it infects Catholicism, may actually be an ecclesiological crisis as much as a media problem, reflecting a growing loss of perspective about what the Church really is and what it's called to be.

The stakes here, in other words, are high. I remain convinced that Catholic journalism is a great calling, not to mention the most absorbing work I can imagine. I believe it deserves better than the culture of contempt, as do the vast majority of my friends and colleagues who produce remarkable reporting despite low pay, strong pressures toward spin and sensationalism, and a frequently chaotic and dysfunctional communications operation in the institutions they cover. I once had a college theology professor who pointed out that although the Church's greatest minds over the centuries have pondered the "problem of evil" at length, there's been comparatively little attention to the "problem of good": How is it that, despite the stain of original sin and the fallen state of the world, so many people, much of the time, nevertheless act for genuinely altruistic and noble motives? That's a great question generally, and it certainly applies with force to the Catholic press.

I can only answer that it's because we recognize that good journalism about the Church is not only professionally satisfying but essential to the Church's own health. That truth may, for the moment, be hard to see sometimes through the fog of contempt. But if Catholicism should teach us anything, it's patience and perspective. This too shall pass—and, if we're imaginative and determined enough, we may be able to play some small role in escorting it off the stage, like all the other distortions of the faith that have had their moment in the sun and then fallen into irrelevance. The Church's natural instinct to find the proper balance between two extremes sooner or later always reasserts itself. If the gates of hell won't prevail against it, neither will the culture of contempt.

Notes

INTRODUCTION

"a noxious brew of anger and disgust": Arthur Brooks, "Our Culture of Contempt," *New York Times*, March 2, 2019, https://www.nytimes.com/2019/03/02/opinion/sunday /political-polarization.html.

"the unsullied conviction of the worthlessness of another": Arthur Brooks, "Our Culture of Contempt," *New York Times*, March 2, 2019, https://www.nytimes.com/2019/03/02 /opinion/sunday/political-polarization.html.

"emotional contagion": Adam D.I. Kramer, Jamie E. Guillory, and Jeffrey T. Hancock, "Experimental evidence of massive-scale emotional contagion through social networks," *PNAS* 111, no. 24 (June 17, 2014): 8788–8790.

false information spreads six times more quickly: Soroush Vosoughi, Deb Roy, and Sinan Aral, "The spread of true and false news online," *Science* 359, no. 6380 (March 9, 2018): 1146–1151.

"Although social media is unlikely to be the main driver of polarization . . .": Jay J. Van Bavel et al., "How social media shapes polarization," *Trends in Cognitive Sciences* 25, no. 11 (November 1, 2021): 913–916.

"significantly reduced polarization of views on policy issues": Hunt Allcott et al., "The Welfare Effects of Social Media," *American Economic Association* 110, no. 3 (March 2020): 629–676.

"Lord Jones is Dead": G.K. Chesterton, *The Wisdom of Father Brown* (New York: Macauley, 1914), 175.

A column in which he suggested I had "dumped" my wife: Michael Voris, "Things Are a Little Amiss in Catholic Media Land," Church Militant, October 30, 2019, https://www .churchmilitant.com/video/episode/vortex-reports-are.

"This tidy little arrangement between Allen and Barron . . .": Michael Voris, "Things Are a Little Amiss in Catholic Media Land," Church Militant, October 30, 2019, https://www .churchmilitant.com/video/episode/vortex-reports-are.

"homosexual predator Satanist": Michael Voris, "Bernardin: Homosexual Predator Satanist," Church Militant, June 26, 2019, https://www.churchmilitant.com/news/article /bernardin-homosexual-predator-satanist.

"With the possible exception of things like box scores, race results, and stock market tabulations . . .": Hunter S. Thompson, *Fear and Loathing: On the Campaign Trail '72* (San Francisco: Straight Arrow, 1973), 44.

"Taliban Catholics": John L. Allen Jr., "A 'Dallas experiment' in orthodoxy and openness," *National Catholic Reporter*, February 5, 2010, https://www.ncronline.org /blogs/all-things-catholic/dallas-experiment-orthodoxy -and-openness.

CHAPTER ONE

iniuria verborum: Thomas Aquinas, *Summa theologiae* 2-2.72.2, trans. Fathers of the English Dominican Province (New York: Benziger Bros., 1947), https://aquinas101 .thomisticinstitute.org.

"I thank you for what you tell us about what is wrong in the Church . . .": Cindy Wooden, "Pope thanks reporters for speaking truth, giving voice to abuse victims," Catholic News Service, November 15, 2021, https://www.ncronline.org

/news/people/pope-thanks-reporters-speaking-truth-giving
-voice-abuse-victims.

The teaching that women cannot be ordained as Catholic priests . . . : Hannah Brockhaus, "Pope Francis reiterates a strong 'no' to women priests," Catholic News Agency, November 1, 2016, https://www.catholicnewsagency.com/news/34847 /pope-francis-reiterates-a-strong-no-to-women-priests.

A 2005 study of Fortune 500 companies: "2005 Catalyst Census of Women Corporate Officers and Top Earners of the Fortune 500 (Report)," Catalyst, July 26, 2006, https:// www.catalyst.org/research/2005-catalyst-census-of-women -corporate-officers-and-top-earners-of-the-fortune-500/.

A 2007 study by the National Association of Women Lawyers: National Association of Women Lawyers, "National Survey on Retention and Promotion of Women in Law Firms," NAWL, November 2007, https://www.nawl.org/p /cm/ld/fid=2019.

CHAPTER TWO

65 percent of American Catholics knew nothing about what Pope Francis had done on the Latin Mass: Gregory A. Smith, "Two-thirds of U.S. Catholics unaware of pope's new restrictions on traditional Latin Mass," Pew Research Center, October 7, 2021, https://www.pewresearch .org/fact-tank/2021/10/07/two-thirds-of-u-s-catholics -unaware-of-popes-new-restrictions-on-traditional-latin -mass/.

traditional jobs in newsrooms across America dropped sharply: Mason Walker, "U.S. newsroom employment has fallen 26% since 2008," Pew Research Center, July 13, 2021, https://www.pewresearch.org/fact-tank/2021/07/13/u-s -newsroom-employment-has-fallen-26-since-2008/.

a critical hiring shortage in TV newsrooms: Andrew Heyward, "The Local Newsroom Recruitment Crisis, Part 1," Knight-Cronkite News Lab, December 30, 2021, https://cronkitenewslab.com/management/2021/12/30/local-newsroom-recruitment-crisis-part-1/.

"demographic winter": Benedict Mayaki, "Pope: Concrete measures needed to revive hope in family and birth," Vatican News, May 12, 2022, https://www.vaticannews.va/en/pope/news/2022-05/pope-general-state-of-birth-natality-cold-demographic-winter.html.

A Baylor University survey: The Baylor Institute for Studies in Religion and the Baylor University Department of Sociology, "American Piety in the 21st Century: New Insights to the Depth and Complexity of Religion in the US," Baylor University website, September 2006, https://www.baylor.edu/content/services/document.php/33304.pdf.

A U.S. News and World Report / PBS Religion and Ethics Newsweekly survey: Mitofsky International and Edison Media Research, "Exploring Religious America," Religion and Ethics Newsweekly, March 26–April 4, 2002, https://www.pbs.org/wnet/religionandethics/2002/04/16/april-26-2002-exploring-religious-america/11558/.

People tend to get more conservative as they age: Sam Peltzman, "Political Ideology over the Life Course," SSRN (December 9, 2019), https://papers.ssrn.com/sol3/papers.cfm?abstract_id=3501174.

"How the community relates to its older members . . .": United States Catholic Bishops, "Blessings of Age," USCCB website, 1999, https://www.usccb.org/topics/marriage-and-family-life-ministries/blessings-age.

FreshySites' most popular Catholic sites in 2022: Ben Giordano, "20 most popular Catholic Church websites for 2022," FreshySites, 2022, https://freshysites.com/focus-on

/parish-website-design/20-most-popular-catholic-church
-websites/.

Feedspot's top Catholic news sites of 2022: "100 Best
Catholic Blogs and Websites," Feedspot, July 18, 2022,
https://blog.feedspot.com/catholic_blogs/.

**63.4 percent of the top ten million websites in 2021 were in
English**: "Usage statistics of content languages for websites,"
W3Techs, https://w3techs.com/technologies/overview
/content_language.

**66 percent of the top 250 YouTube channels were in
English**: Brian Yang, "6 Common Features Of Top 250
YouTube Channels," Twinword, https://www.twinword.com
/blog/features-of-top-250-youtube-channels/.

**Mother Angelica's main competitor in building a national
Catholic television network . . . :** Heidi Schlumpf, "How
Mother Angelica's 'miracle of God' became a global media
empire," *National Catholic Reporter*, July 19, 2019, https://
www.ncronline.org/news/media/how-mother-angelicas
-miracle-god-became-global-media-empire.

**"a large Catholic television channel that has no hesitation
in continually speaking ill of the pope"**: Antonio Spadaro,
"'Freedom Scares Us': Pope Francis' conversation with Slovak
Jesuits," La Civiltà Cattolica, October 20, 2021, https://
www.laciviltacattolica.com/freedom-scares-us-pope-francis
-conversation-with-slovak-jesuits/.

**the influential blogger Fr. Z posted an entry about a priest
in Chicago**: John Zuhlsdorf, "Exceptionally cringeworthy:
Fr. Jackass and his final 'rock on' guitar blessing," *Fr. Z's
Blog*, February 20, 2022, https://wdtprs.com/2022/02
/exceptionally-cringeworthy-fr-jackass-and-his-final-rock-on
-guitar-blessing/.

Its original name was Real Catholic TV, but Voris changed it in 2012: "On Claims of 'Disobedience,'" Church Militant, https://www.churchmilitant.com/main/generic /on-claims-of-disobedience.

LifeSite's Twitter and Facebook accounts have been temporarily suspended: David McLoone, "Twitter suspends two LifeSite accounts for calling 'transgender woman' a man," January 25, 2021, LifeSite News, https://www .lifesitenews.com/news/twitter-suspends-two-lifesite -accounts-for-calling-transgender-woman-a-man/; Doug Mainwaring, "BREAKING: Facebook permanently removes LifeSiteNews' page," LifeSite News, May 4, 2021, https://www.lifesitenews.com/news/breaking-facebook -permanently-bans-lifesitenews-page/.

"harbors all kinds of blasphemies while being financed by the church": Cameron Doody, "'Infovaticana' Cries Foul After Taste of Own Medicine," Patheos, March 22, 2018, https:// www.patheos.com/blogs/europeancommunion/2018/03 /infovaticana-vatican-trademark-censorship/.

CHAPTER FOUR

I, Sniper **dialogue**: Stephen Hunter, *I, Sniper* (New York: Simon & Schuster, 2009), 183–184.

"intrinsic moral evil": Joseph Ratzinger, "Letter to the Bishops of the Catholic Church on the Pastoral Care of Homosexual Persons," October 1, 1986, vatican.va.

bishops' conferences have no teaching authority on their own: Joseph Ratzinger with Vittorio Messori, *The Ratzinger Report: An Exclusive Interview on the State of the Church*, trans. Salvator Attanasio and Graham Harrison (San Francisco: Ignatius, 1985), 60–61.

"Not this Nazi we have now": Reuters Staff, "Susan Sarandon calls Pope Benedict a Nazi," Reuters, October 18, 2011, https://www.reuters.com/article/us-susansarandon /susan-sarandon-calls-pope-benedict-a-nazi-report-idUS TRE79G6AY20111018.

"He'll never be able to connect with young people like John Paul . . .": Mark Landler, "New Pope's Birthplace Becomes a Center of Pride, With Muted Misgivings," *New York Times*, April 20, 2005, https://www.nytimes.com/2005/04/20 /world/worldspecial2/new-popes-birthplace-becomes-a -center-of-pride-with.html.

"In the church, priests are also sinners . . .": "Ratzinger on Abuse, Celibacy, Gays," CBS News, April 19, 2005, https:// www.cbsnews.com/news/ratzinger-on-abuse-celibacy-gays/.

CHAPTER FIVE

63 percent of all Americans have a positive impression of Francis: Claire Gecewicz, "Americans, including Catholics, have favorable views of Pope Francis," Pew Research Center, June 25, 2021, https://www.pewresearch.org/fact-tank /2021/06/25/americans-including-catholics-continue-to -have-favorable-views-of-pope-francis/.

Viganò demanded that Francis resign: Ryan Foley, "Archbishop slams Catholic leaders for allowing 'heresy, sodomy and corruption' to run rampant," The Christian Post, July 28, 2020, https://www.christianpost.com/news /archbishop-slams-catholic-leaders-for-allowing-heresy -sodomy-and-corruption-to-run-rampant.html.

Francis never directly responded to Viganò: Junno Arocho Esteves, "Former nuncio claims Vatican official has evidence of cover-up," *National Catholic Reporter*, September 28, 2018, https://www.ncronline.org/news/accountability

/former-nuncio-claims-vatican-official-has-evidence
-cover?site_redirect=1.

Viganò asserted that Francis is guilty of heresy: Ryan Foley,
"Archbishop slams Catholic leaders for allowing 'heresy,
sodomy and corruption' to run rampant," The Christian
Post, July 28, 2020, https://www.christianpost.com/news
/archbishop-slams-catholic-leaders-for-allowing-heresy
-sodomy-and-corruption-to-run-rampant.html.

**Viganò issued a lengthy statement on the Russian invasion
of Ukraine**: Carlo Maria Viganò, "Declaration on the Russia
-Ukraine Crisis," Inside the Vatican, March 7, 2022, https://
insidethevatican.com/news/newsflash/letter-45-2022
-mon-mar-7-vigano/.

He's also expanded his reach into secular politics: Carlo Maria
Viganò, "Open Letter to the President of the United States
of America," LifeSite News, October 25, 2020, https://www
.lifesitenews.com/news/abp-vigano-warns-trump-about
-great-reset-plot-to-subdue-humanity-destroy-freedom/.

Correctio filialis de haeresibus propagates: *Correctio filialis
de haeresibus propagates*, Catholic Culture, July 16, 2017,
https://www.catholicculture.org/culture/library/view.cfm
?recnum=11665.

**"For more than fifty years heretical, evil theologians
have tried to conquer power . . .":** Andrea Tornielli, "Livi's
anathema: 'Heretics and wicked men are in power in the
Church,'" *La Stampa*, July 3, 2018, https://www.lastampa.it
/vatican-insider/en/2018/07/03/news/livi-s-anathema-heretics
-and-wicked-men-are-in-power-in-the-church-1.34029093.

**this round-up of the sort of thing that's routinely in the
Catholic ether . . . :** Dwight Longenecker, "Radical Catholic
blogs may be a cesspool, but saying so won't help," Crux,
May 27, 2016, https://cruxnow.com/church/2016/05/radical
-catholic-blogs-may-be-a-cesspool-but-saying-so-wont-help.

"supreme, full, immediate, and universal ordinary power in the church": Code of Canon Law §331, vatican.va.

Francis issued legal degrees known as "rescripts" . . . : Andrea Gagliarducci, "Vatican finance trial: What's happened so far and where is it heading?" Catholic News Agency, November 17, 2021, https://www.catholicnewsagency.com /news/249608/vatican-finance-trial-what-s-happened-so-far -and-where-is-it-heading.

CHAPTER SIX

the left-of-center Italian newspaper *Il Fatto Quotidiano* set off a blaze . . . : Loris Mazzetti, "Papa Francesco, il vescovo ciellino di Ferrara: 'Bergoglio deve fare la fine dell'altro Pontefice,'" *Il Fatto Quotidiano*, November 25, 2015, https:// www.ilfattoquotidiano.it/2015/11/25/papa-francesco -vescovo-cl-di-ferrara-bergoglio-deve-fare-la-fine-dellaltro -pontefice/2251753/.

Negri was also perceived as a staunch opponent of abortion . . . : Rick Noack, "Abortions caused Italy's economic crisis, archbishop claims," *Washington Post*, February 5, 2015, https://www.washingtonpost.com/news/worldviews /wp/2015/02/05/abortions-caused-italys-economic-crisis -archbishop-claims/; "Italian prelate who supposedly wanted Pope Francis dead resigns," Crux, February 15, 2017, https://cruxnow.com/global-church/2017/02/italian -prelate-supposedly-wanted-pope-francis-dead-resigns.

the full text of Mazzetti's report: Loris Mazzetti, "Papa Francesco, il vescovo ciellino di Ferrara: 'Bergoglio deve fare la fine dell'altro Pontefice,'" *Il Fatto Quotidiano*, November 25, 2015, https://www.ilfattoquotidiano.it/2015/11/25 /papa-francesco-vescovo-cl-di-ferrara-bergoglio-deve-fare-la -fine-dellaltro-pontefice/2251753/.

Negri insisted that the article was based on "inventions" . . . : "Italian prelate who supposedly wanted Pope Francis dead resigns," Crux, February 15, 2017, https://cruxnow.com/global-church/2017/02/italian-prelate-supposedly-wanted-pope-francis-dead-resigns.

CHAPTER SEVEN

LifeSite often features the writings of Archbishop Carlo Maria Viganò: Carlo Maria Viganò, "Abp. Viganò: Globalists have fomented war in Ukraine to establish the tyranny of the New World Order," LifeSite News, March 7, 2022, https://www.lifesitenews.com/opinion/abp-vigano-globalists-have-fomented-war-in-ukraine-to-establish-the-tyranny-of-the-new-world-order/.

"establish a powerful cabal to force the normalization of homosexuality and transgenderism within the Catholic Church in the United States": Doug Mainwaring, "Petition demands Fr. James Martin not be considered for Philadelphia archbishop," LifeSite News, November 27, 2019, https://www.lifesitenews.com/blogs/petition-demands-fr-james-martin-not-be-considered-for-philadelphia-archbishop/.

"I am against abortion . . .": Raymond Gravel, "Raymond Gravel on Unborn Victims of Crime Act," Open Parliament website, March 3, 2008, https://openparliament.ca/debates/2008/3/3/raymond-gravel-1/only/.

"heretical and anti-life statements": John-Henry Westen, "Editorial: Canadian Catholic Priest Politician Condemns LifeSiteNews.com Founders in Parliament," LifeSite News, March 4, 2008, https://www.lifesitenews.com/news/editorial-canadian-catholic-priest-politician-condemns-founders-in-parliament/.

"One finds herein the remarkably complex phenomenon . . .": "Toronto priest plagiarized when ghostwriting for Canada's most senior Vatican figure: new book," *National Post*, August 27, 2020, https://nationalpost.com/news/new-revelations-in -the-serial-plagiarism-of-a-canadian-priest-extend-to-his-role -as-ghostwriter-for-vatican-figure.

He was also forced to issue a series of public apologies: "Rosica resigns from Salt and Light after plagiarism scandal," Catholic News Agency, June 18, 2019, https:// www.catholicnewsagency.com/news/41576/rosica-resigns -from-salt-and-light-after-plagiarism-scandal.

In a 2013 interview with Sirius XM's "The Catholic Channel" . . . : John-Henry Westen, "Editorial: Salt and Light's Fr. Rosica says LifeSiteNews is Doing 'the work of Satan,'" LifeSite News, September 14, 2009, https://www .lifesitenews.com/news/editorial-salt-and-lights-fr-rosica-says -lifesitenews-is-doing-the-work-of-/.

"low credibility" rating: "LifeSiteNews," Media Bias/Fact Check website, November 25, 2016, https://mediabiasfact check.com/life-site-news/.

"propaganda tools": Joseph Mercola, "Here's how 'fact -checkers' and the media have collaborated to control the public's perception of reality," LifeSiteNews, February 10, 2022, https://www.lifesitenews.com/opinion/heres-how-fact -checkers-and-the-media-have-collaborated-to-control-the -publics-perception-of-reality/.

LifeSite has also faced sanctions on several social media platforms: David McLoone, "Twitter suspends two Life-Site accounts for calling 'transgender woman' a man," LifeSite News, January 25, 2021, https://www.lifesitenews .com/news/twitter-suspends-two-lifesite-accounts-for -calling-transgender-woman-a-man/; Doug Mainwaring, "BREAKING: Facebook permanently removes LifeSiteNews'

page," LifeSite News, May 4, 2021, https://www.lifesitenews
.com/news/breaking-facebook-permanently-bans-lifesite
news-page/.

CHAPTER EIGHT

"historic and exhilarating": "Statement of Archbishop
Charles J. Chaput, O.F.M. Cap. Regarding Pope Francis'
Announcement That He Will Attend the World Meeting of
Families—Philadelphia 2015," Archdiocese of Philadelphia
Schools, November 18, 2014, https://aopcatholicschools
.org/2014/11/18/statement-of-archbishop-charles-j-chaput-o
-f-m-cap-regarding-pope-francis-announcement-that-he-will
-attend-the-world-meeting-of-families-philadelphia-2015/.

"embodies the message of mercy, joy and love that lies at
the heart of the Gospel": "Remarks of Archbishop Charles
Chaput, O.F.M. Cap. at News Conference Announcing the
Theme for the World Meeting of Families – Philadelphia
2015," Archdiocese of Philadelphia, May 13, 2014, https://
archphila.org/remarks-of-archbishop-charles-j-chaput-o-f
-m-cap-at-news-conference-announcing-the-theme-for-the
-world-meeting-of-families-philadelphia-2015/.

"absolutely no credibility": Matthew Gambino, "Archbishop
Chaput to pope: Cancel youth synod, meet about
bishops," Catholic Philly, August 31, 2018, https://catholic
philly.com/2018/08/news/local-news/archbishop
-chaput-to-pope-cancel-youth-synod-meet-about-bishops
/comment-page-1/.

"I thought the church in Philadelphia needed leadership
for the future and I just couldn't do that because of my
age": Pablo Kay, "'The Holy Spirit always wins in the end':
An interview with Archbishop Chaput," Angelus News,
March 26, 2021, https://angelusnews.com/arts-culture

/the-holy-spirit-always-wins-in-the-end-an-interview-with
-archbishop-chaput/.

**"I admit that I find it tiresome to have to continually
criticize Archbishop Chaput . . .":** Michael Sean Winters,
"Archbishop Chaput's regrettable column," *National Catholic
Reporter*, August 15, 2016, https://www.ncronline.org/blogs
/distinctly-catholic/archbishop-chaputs-regrettable-column.

**"Publicly denying Communion to public officials is not
always wise or the best pastoral course . . .":** Charles
Chaput, "Mr. Biden and the Matter of Scandal," *First Things*,
December 4, 2020, https://www.firstthings.com/web
-exclusives/2020/12/mr-biden-and-the-matter-of-scandal.

a bristling response from Winters: Michael Sean Winters,
"American Viganò: Archbishop Chaput divides episcopacy
even in retirement," *National Catholic Reporter*, December
9, 2020, https://www.ncronline.org/news/opinion/distinctly
-catholic/american-vigan-archbishop-chaput-divides
-episcopacy-even-retirement.

**"devout schismatics . . . [who] openly promote the under-
mining of the bishop of Rome among the Catholic faithful":**
Massimo Faggioli, "The rise of 'devout schismatics' in the
Catholic Church," La Croix International, August 15,
2019, https://international.la-croix.com/news/religion
/the-rise-of-devout-schismatics-in-the-catholic-church/10535.

**"public record has shown some very clear signs of resistance
to—and even subversion of—Pope Francis and his
teachings":** Mike Lewis, "The Archbishop Doth Protest Too
Much," *Where Peter Is*, July 22, 2019, https://wherepeteris.
com/the-archbishop-doth-protest-too-much/.

**"As a bishop, the only honest way I can talk about the
abuse tragedy is to start by apologizing for the failure of the
Church and her leaders . . .":** Charles J. Chaput, "Launching
the Fortnight for Freedom," *First Things*, June 21, 2012,

https://www.firstthings.com/web-exclusives/2012/06
/launching-the-fortnight-for-freedom.

**"enjoyed working with Archbishop Viganò during his
tenure as Apostolic Nuncio"**: Mary Farrow, "Vigano
testimony receives mixed response from US bishops,"
Catholic News Agency, August 27, 2018, https://www
.catholicnewsagency.com/news/39239/vigano-testimony
-receives-mixed-response-from-us-bishops.

**"an eccentric businessman of defective ethics whose
bombast and buffoonery make him inconceivable as
president"**: Charles Chaput, "Some personal thoughts on
the months ahead," Catholic Philly, August 12, 2016, https://
catholicphilly.com/2016/08/archbishop-chaput-column
/some-personal-thoughts-on-the-months-ahead/.

"profoundly bad idea": "Archbishop Chaput's Address at
Panel Discussion on Immigration: Sanity, Indifference
and the American Immigration Debate," Archdiocese
of Philadelphia, September 2, 2015, https://archphila
.org/2389-2/.

**"There's a human cost to political theater that can be
inexcusably ugly . . ."**: Charles Chaput, "A great nation, if
we act accordingly," Catholic Philly, June 22, 2018, https://
catholicphilly.com/2018/06/archbishop-chaput-column/a
-great-nation-if-we-act-accordingly/.

**"illegal immigration as well—which is supported in
order to destabilize nations . . ."**: Carlo Maria Viganò (@
ArchbpVigano), Twitter, March 15, 2021, 6:42 a.m., https://
twitter.com/ArchbpVigano/status/1371411560413892610.

**"What the death penalty does achieve is closure through
bloodletting, and violence against violence . . ."**: Charles
Chaput, "Archbishop Chaput's Weekly Column: The Death
Penalty, Again," Archdiocese of Philadelphia, August 2,

2019, https://archphila.org/archbishop-chaputs-weekly
-column-the-death-penalty-again/.

"I buried some of the young Columbine victims twenty years ago . . .": Charles Chaput, "Archbishop Chaput's Weekly Column: Gilroy, El Paso, Dayton—and Columbine," Archdiocese of Philadelphia, August 5, 2019, https://archphila.org/archbishop-chaputs-weekly-column-gilroy-el-paso-dayton-and-columbine/.

"As I got older, I began to see that there was no integrity . . .": "Archbishop Chaput: Some Catholic bishops were 'too compliant' with pandemic restrictions," Catholic News Agency, June 3, 2021, https://www.catholicnewsagency.com/news/247881/archbishop-chaput-some-catholic-bishops-were-too-compliant-with-pandemic-restrictions.

"The sole desire of both Lepanto and Church Militant is to create division . . .": Matt C. Abbott, "Philly archbishop labels two Catholic groups 'destructive'," RenewAmerica, August 27, 2015, http://www.renewamerica.com/columns/abbott/150827.

"too compliant": "Archbishop Chaput: Some Catholic bishops were 'too compliant' with pandemic restrictions," Catholic News Agency, June 3, 2021, https://www.catholicnewsagency.com/news/247881/archbishop-chaput-some-catholic-bishops-were-too-compliant-with-pandemic-restrictions.

Viganò is an acerbic critic of the Second Vatican Council: Carlo Maria Vigano, "Interview with Phil Lawler," Catholic Culture, June 2020, https://www.catholicculture.org/culture/library/view.cfm?recnum=12379.

"I think the Second Vatican Council is the most precious gift . . .": Pablo Kay, "'The Holy Spirit always wins in the end': An interview with Archbishop Chaput," Angelus News, March 26, 2021, https://angelusnews.com/arts-culture

/the-holy-spirit-always-wins-in-the-end-an-interview-with
-archbishop-chaput/.

CONCLUSION

some of this content was strong medicine: Dwight
Longenecker, "'Amoris Laetitia': Are we seeing change by
stealth?" Crux, January 19, 2017, https://cruxnow.com
/vatican/2017/01/amoris-laetitia-seeing-change-stealth;
"From a communications point of view, 'Amoris Laetitia' is
a shipwreck," Crux, August 23, 2017, https://cruxnow.com
/commentary/2017/08/communications-point-view-amoris
laetitia-shipwreck; Austen Ivereigh, "Papal confidante says
'Amoris' critics locked in 'death-trap' logic," Crux, August
21, 2017, https://cruxnow.com/vatican/2017/08/21/papal
-confidante-says-amoris-critics-locked-death-trap-logic;
"Pope Francis and the convert problem," Crux, August
9, 2017, https://cruxnow.com/commentary/2017/08/09
/pope-francis-convert-problem.

**"The venomous and vitriolic bloggers will most assuredly
not accept criticism . . .":** Dwight Longenecker, "Radical
Catholics blogs may be a cesspool, but saying so won't help,"
Crux, May 27, 2016, https://cruxnow.com/church/2016/05
/radical-catholic-blogs-may-be-a-cesspool-but-saying-so
-wont-help.

**CBS and MSNBC both suspended Imus and then canceled
his show:** "CBS Fires Don Imus Over Racial Slur," CBS
News, April 12, 2007, https://www.cbsnews.com/news
/cbs-fires-don-imus-over-racial-slur/.